POCKET HISTORY OF
Irish Saints

Brian Lacey

THE O'BRIEN PRESS
DUBLIN

First published 2003 by The O'Brien Press Ltd,
20 Victoria Road, Dublin 6, Ireland.
Tel: +353 1 4923333; Fax: +353 1 4922777
E-mail: books@obrien.ie
Website: www.obrien.ie

ISBN: 0-86278-746-7

British Library Cataloguing-in-Publication Data
A catalogue record for this title is available from
the British Library

1 2 3 4 5 6
03 04 05 06 07

The O'Brien Press receives
assistance from

Editin ...

Printing: C...

Front co... of Muiredach's Cross, Monasterboice, County Louth.
Photog... ... the H...

Commis ...
p.5; Nat ...

Contents

Introduction

A book about saints may seem a bit esoteric, even some-what passé, at the beginning of the twenty-first century. Yet, recently, the relics of St Thérèse of Lisieux were brought on tour around Ireland and it is claimed that over two million visits were made to see them. Despite the recent decline in religious belief and practices, saints are still very much part of the common social and cultural fabric of modern Ireland. This is similar to the situation in many other countries in Europe and elsewhere, particularly those in which Catholi-cism has been the dominant religious identity.

In Ireland, the official titles of places, educational institu-tions, hospitals, cultural and sporting bodies and charitable organisations often include the name of a well-known saint. In the Republic of Ireland, the holiday after Christmas is offi-cially called St Stephen's Day, and many other days of the year are known, or in the past *were* known, by the name of the saint whose 'feast day' occurs on that date. Some of these saints are international figures, drawn from the history of the universal Christian Church, but most are local – par-ticular to Ireland, or even to small districts of the country.

What is a saint? Oscar Wilde, who by all accounts thought of himself as a sort of martyred saint, said: 'Love can canon-ise people. The saints are those who have been most loved.' The concept of the 'saint' is not unique to Christianity. Broadly similar ideas can be found in some of the other great religious cultures of the world, such as in Hinduism and Islam. The English word 'saint' is derived from the Latin *sanctus* meaning holy or sacred – dedicated to the service of God. The idea has a very ancient history. In the New Testa-ment, St Paul uses the word to describe all the believers in Christ, rather than particular individuals. That idea is still retained in the Feast of All Saints, celebrated each year on 1 November, when all those who are believed to have 'died in Christ' and 'gone to Heaven' are remembered officially by the church.

During the first and second centuries, the word 'saint' began to be applied as a mark of honour to particular individuals, especially to the early martyrs and the first monks. Associated with this development was the growth of devotional practices and commemorative services in honour of the person in question. Also, the names of these saints began to be given to children at baptism as a mark of honour and dedication. Another aspect of this process was the reverence given to 'relics' (from Latin *reliquiae,* 'to leave behind') – objects associated with the saint or, even more importantly, parts of their bodily remains. The word in modern Irish for a graveyard – *reilig* – derives from this same idea.

From the second century, anniversaries of the saints' deaths were being commemorated; not as days of mourning but as 'feast days', the *dies natalis* (literally 'birthday'), the day the saint was believed to have been reborn into the next life. Again from earliest times, abuses and superstitions began to develop around the names of the saints. Relics and various other objects said to be associated with the saints were often used, harmlessly enough, for 'blessings'. More controversially, some of these objects were also used for 'cursings'. Such practices have been a continuing source of problems for the Christian Church, not least here in Ireland, down to modern times. They were a particular bugbear of the promoters of the Protestant Reformation, who argued that some of these practices came close to (and may, indeed, have actually been, at least in origin) acts of worship. For this reason, many of the 'reformed' churches abandoned the practices associated with saints altogether. The

Roman Catholic Church was obliged to deal with these allegations in a variety of ways. Local saints' 'pattern', or patron, days, which were often accompanied by notorious feats of merrymaking and drinking, were often suppressed by the Catholic clergy in Ireland, particularly in the second half of the nineteenth century.

With the acceptance of Christianity by the Roman Emperor Constantine in the early fourth century, the age of persecution and martyrdom of believers came to an end. As a consequence, by the close of that century, the concept of the 'saint' had been extended. It could now include the hermits known as the 'desert fathers', as well as distinguished bishops and church teachers. These saints, who had not been martyred for their faith, became known in the later church as the 'confessors'.

Along with the development of the idea of the saint came the production of hagiography (from Greek *hagios*, 'holy', and *graphein*, 'to write') – the writing of 'Lives' of the saints. The earliest examples of these consist of sermons for delivery on the saint's feast day, but they soon developed into the more extensive *Acta* ('Acts') and *Vitae* ('Lives') of the saints. These were works intended more to excite veneration than to be biographies in our modern sense. They were designed not to give the biographical facts of a saint's life but, in the words of Irish scholar Ailbhe Mac Shamhráin, to enlarge 'the reputation of the subject'. The academic study of the hagiography of Irish saints often reveals major discrepancies between what we can know about a saint's actual historical life and his or her hagiographical 'Life'.

A saint is known to be a saint by virtue of having been canonised, that is, their name has been added to a 'canon', or list, of saints. This began as an informal, spontaneous, even democratic process but, as Christianity became increasingly institutionalised, canonisation became the prerogative of the bishop or leader of a local church. From the tenth century, the decision began to be reserved more and more for the bishop of Rome, the pope. Under Pope Alexander III, who died in 1181, a formal process of canonisation was introduced, and restricted to the papacy. Initial moves towards canonisation often continued (and, indeed, still do continue) to arise among the laity, much in the way that popular acclamation occurred in the early Church.

In the Roman Catholic Church, as part of the Counter-Reformation response to the emergence of Protestantism, a more elaborate and formal system came into use as a result of edicts in 1625 and 1634 by Pope Urban VIII. A systematic investigation of the life of the candidate for canonisation was now required, as was proof of the occurrence of relevant miracles through the 'intercession' of the person in question. The process was further modified and refined in the 1740s, and again by Pope John Paul II in 1983. The Christian Orthodox churches have a somewhat similar, if less rigid, system but, whereas some Protestant churches, such as the Church of Ireland, retain some of the traditions associated with the early saints, they have not continued the practice of canonisation. Of course, in the eyes of the Christian Church, the process of canonisation does not 'make' a saint; it is merely a formal declaration that the individual in question 'was' a saint during their own lifetime.

By the time that Christianity came to Ireland, probably in the fifth century, the idea of the Christian saint had been fully worked out. It seems, however, that this aspect of Christianity came to be more highly developed in this country – so much so that in the middle ages the title *Insula Sanctorum*, the 'Island of Saints', came to be used as a poetic name for Ireland. This Irish reputation for saints was well established in continental Europe in the early middle ages. The humorist critic, Hubert Butler, wrote an amusing book called *Ten Thousand Saints: a Study in Irish and European Origins* (1972), highlighting the excess of Irish saints. It does seem true that elevation to sainthood was more common here than in many other places. A list in the twelfth-century *Book of Leinster* names about 1,100 Irish 'saints', and the historian John Ryan reckoned that the medieval Irish martyrologies, texts that list saints chronologically according to the dates of their feast days, contained the names of about 1,700 saints from this country. Not all of these – indeed, not many, as we will see – would stand up to the rigorous historical investigation required since 1634. Most Irish saints belong to the ranks of those unofficially canonised. In fact, despite the numbers claimed above, only four Irish individuals have been officially canonised by the Church.

Irish saints of the early Christian period are still commemorated in the names of places (for example, Ardpatrick, Desertmartin, Glencolumbkille, Kilkieran, Mount Brandon, Skellig Michael, and so on), as well as in ancient ecclesiastical sites, in holy wells and 'rag bushes' beside such wells, where cures are believed to take place, and even in unusual topographical features. Stories about the saints in local folklore are often given very precise locations in the landscape, which can still be pointed out as much as 1,500 years after the alleged events. For example, St Kevin's Bed in Glendalough, St Patrick's Purgatory in Lough Derg, Lacknacoo in Gartan in Donegal – the very stone on which Colum Cille is said to have been born – as well as a host of various saints' knee-prints, hand-prints and foot-prints, embedded in prominent and revered rocks.

Indeed, this localisation of the saint (appropriating him or her as a local hero, local patron, local healer, etc.) is one of the most characteristic features of the traditions associated with the saints in Ireland. The practice of this in the past has left us with a lot of confusion over the real identity of particular saints. It seems that the practice persists. I recently heard a young Dublin boy on the radio referring to the contemporary tour of relics of the saint from Lisieux in France as belonging to 'St Thérèse of Leixlip'. Such errors have a long history.

Early literature about the saints in Ireland is vast. It includes material such as martyrologies, genealogies and pedigrees, poems and anecdotes and, most importantly of all, the saints' Lives, both in Latin (*Vitae*) and in Irish (*Bethada*). These Lives are largely works of fiction, 'constructing' the saint in the image required by the authors for their contemporary purposes. Liam de Paor, who studied many of them, says in his book *Saint Patrick's World*:

> ... the saints Life became a kind of code, to exalt its hero or heroine in competition with others, to impress (and entertain) by marvels, to define rights and claims of the church to which the saint (usually as founder) belonged and its relationship with other churches, and, sometimes, to extol the power and virtue of the saint's relics, held in the church shrines ...

> ... saints' Lives were popular writing and catered for the pilgrims to the monastic shrines: a form of promotional literature directed partly at early medieval tourists. They also served, however, and it was an important part of their function, as evidence for the rights, rents, and dues of the churches and of the relationships in primacy and property between churches ...

Another scholar, Kathleen Hughes, commenting on these more secular aspects, said that the Lives were 'often determined to boost the saint's claims at any cost to his moral stature'. Indeed, some of the actions of our saints as depicted in the Lives were not particularly 'saintly'. In the twelfth century, the Norman writer Gerald of Wales wrote in his book *The History and Topography of Ireland* of: 'Vindictiveness, in which the saints of this country seem to be very interested.'

A document known as the *Catalogue of the Saints of Ireland*, which was probably written in the eighth century, classifies the Irish saints up to the year 665 (the year of the Great Plague). Three classes or 'orders' are specified. *Ordo sanctissimus* (the 'holiest') are said to date to between the time of Saint Patrick and the year 544, when there was another plague.

> The first order of Catholic saints, was in the time of Patrick; and then they were all bishops, distinguished and holy, and full of the Holy Ghost, 350 in number, founders of churches. They had one head, Christ, and one chief, Patrick. They had one Mass, one liturgy, one tonsure from ear to ear. They celebrated one Easter, on the fourteenth moon after the vernal equinox, and what was excommunicated by one church all excommunicated. They did not reject the service and society of women because founded on a rock, Christ, they feared not the blast of temptation. This order of saints lasted for four reigns, those namely of [high kings] Laoghaire, Ailill Molt, Lugaid son of Laoghaire and Tuathal. All these bishops are sprung from the Romans and Franks and Britons and Irish.

The second order, *Ordo sanctior* ('holier'), consists of 300 saints. These are said to have lived in the period between 545 and 598. The third order is *Ordo sanctus* ('holy') and includes 100 saints who lived, allegedly, between 599 and 664.

Martyrologies, or lists of saints, are also called Calendars (the word in Irish is *Félire* – 'calendar' in the modern language). Three such documents survive from the early medieval period in Ireland: the *Martyrology of Oengus*, probably written around 800; the *Martyrology of Tallaght*, probably written in the early tenth century; and the *Martyrology of Gorman*, probably written around the year 1170. A fourth text, the *Martyrology of Donegal*, was compiled by Brother Michael O'Clery in the 1620s.

The scientific study of saints' Lives began in what is now Belgium, in the late sixteenth century. A group of Jesuit scholars, who later became known as the Bollandists, set about collecting and studying the *Acta Sanctorum* or 'Acts of the Saints'. About the same time, a group of Irish scholars, mainly associated with the Irish Franciscan college in Louvain, began a similar endeavour. One of the most assiduous of the Irish researchers was the Brother Michael O'Clery mentioned above but, perhaps, the best known of these pioneering scholars was Fr John Colgan, from Inishowen in Donegal. He published two major volumes of annotated saints' Lives: the *Acta Sanctorum Hiberniae* in 1645, comprising material relating to the Irish saints commemorated in the calendar from 1 January to 31 March, and the *Trias Thaumaturga* ('Three Miracleworkers') in 1647, which collected together Lives and other material relating to Saints Patrick, Brigid and Colum Cille, the three patron saints of ancient and medieval Ireland.

Modern secular scholars continue to study the Lives of the saints, sometimes challenging strongly held local traditions and beliefs. A good example of this is the work of Pádraig Ó Riain. In a series of works, Ó Riain argued – to some local controversy – that the stories of Saint Finbarr of Cork are really 'a local version of an otherwise very widely diffused cult which originated with Finbarr, alias Finnian, patron and probable founder of the church of Moville, near Bangor in County Down.' Ó Riain has also shown that many saints with the same name, listed in the various sources as separate individuals, were in reality the same person. The very common early Irish practice of giving hypocoristic (endearing or 'pet' name) forms, and adding diminutive elements – again as a form of endearment – to saints' names has often resulted in a multiplicity of names, apparently of different individuals, but actually referring to the same person:

A priori the notion that there existed hundreds of SS Colmán, scores of SS Mochua and Molaisse and dozens of saints of other denominations [names] within one relatively small area by European standards, in the course of a very limited period of time, again by European standards, flouts the most basic rules of common sense, not to mention historical criticism, no matter which gloss is put on the word saint.

Some scholars have suggested that certain traditions associated with some of the Irish saints may reflect aspects of the religious beliefs of pre-Christian times. Indeed, Ó Riain has said that 'many of the early saints originated as pagan deities'. Certain saintly characters may, either in part or in total, be no more than euhemerised or 'humanised' pagan gods and goddesses. The names of well-known pre-Christian heroes or deities, such as Brigid, Etain, Medbh, Nuadu and Oisín, also appear in the lists of saints. Other saints' names contain elements such as *aed* ('flame') or *las* ('light'), which, to say the least, give rise to suspicion. An apocryphal story tells how when strolling on the beach one day, monks from the ancient monastery of Bangor (now in County Down) came across a mermaid. The monks were anxious to do the right thing for the mermaid and agonised over whether or not to baptise her. After prolonged theological speculation, they decided not only to baptise her, but to canonise her!

An interesting aspect of the study of saints is observing how their cults have grown and expanded over time. This has come about as new Lives have been written, as devotion to a saint has spread geographically, and as new stories, new sites and new practices have been absorbed into a cult. Secular political support can also play its part. We see this in the rise of the cult of St Patrick with the strong support of the politically important Uí Néill dynasty. St Brigid's cult was enhanced through the support of the Uí Dúnlainge kings of Leinster. Also, a very important aspect of the cult of a saint was the practices surrounding his or her feast day; Irish saints, however, had, as one historian has said, the disconcerting habit of often having a multiplicity of feast days.

It would take a much bigger book than this to discuss the more than 1,000 Irish saints for whom some sort of tradition exists. Only a select few will be described below, chosen because of their inherent importance or because significant literary sources for them are available.

This account is, of course, indebted to the work of many scholars. Despite having been published originally in 1929, a major source for the study of the early Irish saints remains J F Kenny's *Sources for the Early History of Ireland: Vol I, Ecclesiastical*. Several of the saints' Lives mentioned below have been translated and discussed in Liam de Paor's *Saint Patrick's World*. An easily available source for St Colum Cille and a number of the saints associated with him is Richard Sharpe's *Adomnán of Iona: Life of St Columba*. A new book which examines many aspects of this subject in an academic way is *Studies in Irish Hagiography: Saints and Scholars*, edited by John Carey, Máire Herbert and Pádraig Ó Riain. These, and the names of other specialist scholars, will be mentioned again below in the appropriate places.

A Note on Dates

Strictly speaking, we can only talk about the 'history' of something when we have contemporary written documentation that describes it. The change from 'prehistory' to 'history', i.e. the introduction of writing, coincides in Ireland with the introduction of Christianity and the beginning of the 'age of the saints'. However, many of the individuals referred to in this book lived at a very early stage in that history. Accurate dating for this period is very difficult, as contemporary written evidence, although existing to some extent, is still relatively scarce. Among our best sources are the texts known as the 'annals'. These are documents into which references to events are entered in chronological order, year by year – hence the name annals. The annals have a complex history of composition, to some extent resembling modern scrapbooks. For instance, it is not yet known for certain when the practice of keeping such annals actually began. In addition, the relationship between the various Irish collections of annals is not yet fully understood. This is important, as the separate collections of annals often record the same event but under different years and with differing details.

In the text below, emphasis will be given to the *Annals of Ulster*, compiled in the late fifteenth and early sixteenth centuries but containing copies of much older material, and the *Annals of Tigernach*, which, although surviving only in a manuscript of the fourteenth century, contains information for the periods 489–766 and 974–1178. Until recently, the *Annals of Ulster* was understood to be the best source for reconstructing our early history. However, the work of Dr Daniel McCarthy from Trinity College, Dublin, in his 'Chronological Synchronisation of the Irish Annals', now indicates that the chronology set out in the *Annals of Tigernach* gives us a more accurate picture. Where possible, in the text below, I have used the revised chronology made available by Dr McCarthy on the internet at http://www.cs.tcd.ie/Dan.McCarthy/chronology/synchronisms/annals-chron.htm

1. Saints of the Universal Church: John, Stephen and Martin

Throughout the bulk of our history, most of the saints venerated in Ireland were Irish themselves. However, a small group of saints belonging to the universal Christian Church did make an impact on the imagination here, and were commemorated in a variety of ways.

A non-Irish saint whose name was, and still is, widely commemorated in Ireland is **John the Baptist**, the 'forerunner' of Jesus Christ. Unusually, St John's main feast day, 24 June, celebrates his real birthday, rather than his death. That day, known in Ireland as *Féile Naomh Eoin*, was until recently the occasion for a wide range of ritual practices and merrymaking. The festival still continues in some parts of the country, but on nothing like the scale of past celebrations.

Like most Irish festivals, the celebrations began on the evening before – St John's Eve. This was *Oíche an Tine Chnáimh*, 'bonfire night', or *Tine Féil Eoin*, 'St John's fire'. People used to throw weeds into the fire to ensure that they would not grow in the fields, and ashes from the fire would be scattered on crops to ensure fertility. There were many other practices associated with fire, integrated into various customs. People rationalised the various fire ceremonies by claiming that St John the Baptist had been martyred through being burned alive; however, the Gospels tell us that King Herod had him beheaded at the request of Salome. It is clear that these fires derive from some other source.

The origins of many of these customs are almost certainly to be found in ancient ceremonies marking the Summer Solstice, 21 June. The shift by a few days to 24 June is

reminiscent of the similar move away from the Winter Solstice (21 December) to the Christian festival of Christmas.

Around the time of St John's festival it was appropriate
to gather the herb known as St John's wort (*Hypericum
perforatum*). This was used for a wide range of medicinal
purposes, and has made something of a comeback as a
cure in our modern era of stress-related illnesses. St John's
wort was also known, particularly in the Hebrides, as St
Columba's wort, the belief being that Colum Cille always
carried some of it with him as a gesture of honour to John
the Baptist.

There were many holy wells dedicated to St John
around the country, at which pilgrimages and 'patterns'
would be held on his feast day and which were believed to
be the sources of various cures. One of these was at Kil-
mainham in Dublin, where a 'pattern' had been held, at
least, since the middle ages. Apparently, it had become so
rowdy a gathering that it was declared illegal by the Irish
parliament in 1710. We are not sure how ancient these
beliefs and practices were, but there are some indications
that special devotion to St John existed in Ireland from very
early times.

There was general unease throughout Ireland in the year
1096, because the feast of the decollation (beheading) of
John the Baptist, 29 August, fell on a Friday, and because it
was also a leap year. An ancient text known as the *Second
Vision of Adomnán* had predicted that such a coincidence
would bring about great danger. The *Annals of the Four
Masters* says of that year:

> The festival of John fell on Friday this year. The men of Ireland
> were seized with great fear, and the counsel taken by the clergy of
> Ireland, with the *comarba* of St Patrick [i.e. the senior cleric of
> Armagh] at their head, in order to save them from the mortality

> which had been predicted to them from a remote period, was to command all in general to observe three days total fast, from Wednesday to Sunday, every month, and an ordinary fast every day till the end of a year, except on Sundays and great festivals. And they also gave alms and many offerings to God, and many lands were granted to churches and the clergy by kings and princes. And so the men of Ireland were saved for that time from the fire of vengeance.

People may also have been extra cautious in 1096 because, according to the *Annals of Ulster*, the previous year, 1095, had been 'the year of the mortality' when there was 'a great sickness in Ireland that killed many people, from the first of August until the following May' (1096). The dreaded visitation which was expected to descend on the country was known as, among other names, *Scúab a Fánait*, the 'Broom from Fanad', County Donegal (i.e. the 'destructive force from the north'). It was to come as vengeance for the beheading of John the Baptist, the worst crime in human history, according to Irish belief, with the exception of the crucifixion of Christ. Ireland was to be hit by this calamity because, according to the same tradition, it was an Irish druid, Mog Ruith, who had actually decapitated John the Baptist. However, as it happened, nothing especially bad occurred in the year 1096.

Notwithstanding our neighbouring island's tradition of Boxing Day, the day after Christmas is known officially in Ireland (especially in the Republic) as St Stephen's Day. **St Stephen**, known as the first Christian martyr, died about AD35. His story is told in the *Acts of the Apostles*. Stephen, probably a Greek-speaking Jew, was accused by the Jewish Council of being a blasphemer and was subsequently stoned to death. The man who would become known as St Paul was allegedly an observer at Stephen's execution. St Stephen's feast day, 26 December, was celebrated all over Ireland at one time as the day for 'hunting the wren'. The wren, or *dreoilín*, was believed in Irish folklore to have betrayed the existence of Stephen in the bushes where he was hiding from his enemies. Accordingly, the wren had to be hunted and killed. For a few days before 26 December, young men would hunt these small birds. If caught, they would be paraded on St Stephen's Day by the 'wran [wren] boys', who would go round the local houses soliciting gifts and singing some variation of the song:

> The wren, the wren, the king of all birds,
> On St Stephen's Day, he was caught in the furze;
> Though his body was little, his family is great,
> So if it pleases yer honour, give us a treat.

It is not known how far back these customs go in Ireland, but a text dating to around the eleventh century, on the passion, or suffering, of St Stephen and the finding of his body, is found in the early fifteenth-century manuscript known as the *Leabhar Breac*.

Another very early saint who was not Irish and who did not come to Ireland, but who was to have a strong influence on this country, mainly through the circulation of writings about him, was **St Martin of Tours**. One historian has written: 'In Ireland there was a special veneration for Martin as a kind of national apostle.' Martin was born at Sabaria in Pannonia (modern Hungary) about the year 315. The son of a Roman soldier, he was brought up at Pavia in Northern Italy and himself became a cavalryman. Later, in 339, he asked for a discharge – stating, 'I am Christ's soldier' – and went to live in Italy and Dalmatia (part of the former Yugoslavia), before going to live as a hermit on an island off the Ligurian coast in the Gulf of Genoa. He subsequently joined St Hilary at his church at Poitiers in France and later, around 361, founded his own community at Ligugé, just outside the gates of that city. This was the first monastery in France, then known as Gaul.

Martin was made bishop of Tours in 371, but not to everyone's satisfaction. His 'biographer' tells us that many of the other Gallo-Roman bishops, who came from the upper classes, were appalled at his appointment, considering him very unfit to be a bishop, 'with his insignificant appearance, his sordid garments and his disgraceful hair'. Instead of living in Tours, Martin preferred to live a solitary life outside the city. This refuge later became the monastery of Marmoutier, on the banks of the River Loire. Martin is remembered as a very active missionary, travelling into remote rural areas of the country and converting the *pagani* (literally 'country people' – from this Latin word are derived the English words 'peasant' and 'pagan'). He died about 397.

Shortly after his death, a Life of St Martin and other texts about him were written by his younger contemporary, Sulpicius Severus. These texts were among the most popular literature in Europe throughout the medieval period. Martin of Tours was one of the first non-martyrs to be honoured as a saint, and his reputation as the 'father' of monasticism in the western church added to the interest in him in the strongly monastic Irish church. St Martin's Cross is one of the most striking monuments at the Columban monastery on Iona, Scotland: it dates to about AD800. There were many dedications to Martin in Ireland also, such as Desertmartin in County Derry, as well as St Martin's wells in many parts of the country.

Sulpicius Severus's Life and other material about Martin is included in the *Book of Armagh*, along with a collection of material about St Patrick.

Many Irish saints are brought, unchronologically, into association with St Martin or are said to have visited his grave in Tours, sometimes returning to Ireland with a variety of relics. Such a relic was *Soiscél Martain*, the 'Gospel of Martin', one of the treasures of the monastery of Derry. This book is now lost, at least by that name, but recently it has been suggested that it may be identifiable as the manuscript nowadays known as the *Cathach*. There was also a grave-yard in Derry dedicated to Martin.

St Martin had many associations with various farming practices. His feast day, 11 November, was formerly called Martinmas and was widely celebrated right up to the twenti-eth century in Ireland. A common practice on St Martin's Eve was for each family to slaughter an animal, and to sprinkle its blood on the threshold and the four corners of the house to ensure its protection. The size of the animal (i.e. whether it was 'a cow or a cock') depended on the relative wealth of each family, and wealthier people shared out portions of the meat with their poorer neighbours. It seems that the origin of this practice was the necessary slaughter of animals fat-tened after the autumn harvest in order to provide food for the winter ahead.

By tradition no work would be done on St Martin's Day, especially anything that involved turning wheels, such as spinning or particularly milling. A Wexford legend claimed that an apparition of St Martin would march up and down the waves along the coast to ensure that no fishing boats put out to sea on that day. St Martin's summer was a name applied to a season of mild weather often experienced around the middle of November through to the beginning of December.

The name Martin is still, of course, very popular in Ireland, but this may be partly related to devotion to (and maybe even some confusion with) St Martin de Porres, the Peruvian mulatto saint who lived in the late sixteenth and early seventeenth century and whose feast day occurs on 3 November.

2. Irish Saints before St Patrick

Traditionally St Patrick, the 'apostle' and patron saint of Ireland, is said to have converted the country to Christianity in the fifth century. Most of the stories about Patrick are located in the northern half of Ireland. However, there are also strong traditions about a number of saints from the south of the country which challenge this dominant narrative. The Corcu Loegde, an ancient people who lived in what is now west Cork, claimed that it was in their territory that 'the cross was believed in first in Ireland'. Among the so-called pre-Patrician saints are Ibar, Declan of Ardmore and Ailbe of Emly.

No separate Life of **St Ibar** survives, but we know from other sources that he was believed to have been the founder of a church on the significantly named Beggery Island (*Becc-Ériu* or 'Little Ireland') in Wexford Harbour. The ruins of a small church can still be found there, although this former island is now joined to the adjacent mainland as a result of reclamation. Ibar is said to have been the most obstinate of the saints when it came to challenging the chronological primacy of St Patrick. As with so many of the Irish 'saints', very little, beyond his name, is actually known about him. In fact, the distinguished historian RAS Macalister even challenged our knowledge of his name, pointing out that *ibar* was the word in old Irish for a yew tree, and that the reference might originally have been to a sacred yew tree of pagan times. Macalister, in an article published in the *Proceedings of the Royal Irish Academy* in 1919, added that another island close to Beggery was known as *Dair Inis* ('Oak Island'), and that Beggery might originally have had an alternative name analogous to this, such as *Inis Ibair* or 'Island of the yew tree'. Macalister continued:

> Let it be clearly understood that the historicity of these saints is not in question. That is amply attested by the existence of the ruins of the religious houses associated with them. But their names have suffered the usual fate of names handed down by tradition, and have become confused with other names which by reason of a much longer history, stretching back into the unknown abysses of pagan ages, had made a deeper impression on popular memory.

The *Annals of Tigernach* records the death of a Bishop Iubair (or Ibar) in 502, so, if the traditions about Ibar reflect history to any extent, we can almost certainly assign the main part of his life to the second half of the fifth century. His feast day is 23 April.

Ibar is said to have had a sister, Milla, who was the wife of Cormac, the king of Leinster. They had a son named Abbán, who is also remembered in tradition as a very early saint. In the Lives, **St Abbán** is associated with St Ibar, St Patrick, the churches of Killabban in County Laois and Moyarney near New Ross in County Wexford, and with other churches and monasteries. Abbán is not a proper name; one explanation is that it means something like 'little abbot' or 'dearest abbot'. Abbán is said to have baptised St Finnian of Clonard. The feast day of Abbán of Moyarney is 27 October, while that of Abbán of Killabban is 16 March, but they may well be the same person and, indeed, may also be identical with the saint discussed below.

St Ailbe (in Latin, Albeus) of Emly, County Tipperary, is another ecclesiastic whose mission was claimed to be earlier than, or independent of, Patrick. He was the patron saint of Munster and his church at Emly was that province's chief ecclesiastical centre. An old saying about him states: 'Let humble Ailbe be the Patrick of Munster.' Ailbe's Life has several mythological associations. His church at Emly, *Imblech Ibair*, takes its name, 'the lakeside at the yew tree', from a (perhaps sacred) pre-Christian yew tree. In some versions of his Life, Ailbe's father is named Ol-chú, 'Great Hound', and Ailbe itself was the name of a divine war-hound which guarded the borders of the kingdom of Leinster as well as other boundaries. There was a place in Leinster called Magh Ailbe, 'Plain of Ailbe', on which stood the Lia Ailbe, 'Standing Stone of Ailbe', named after this famous hound.

Ancient etymologists derived the name of Ailbe of Emly from the Irish words *Ail* (rock) and *beo* (living), based on the story of his birth. Ailbe's mother was a slave of a king. The king had ordered that her baby be killed. Instead, he was hidden under a rock, *Ail*, and found alive, *beo*, there by a wolf who 'like a gentle mother, fondly nourished him among her own cubs.' Near the end of his life we are told that he repaid this kindness when a she-wolf who was being chased with her companions by hunters fled to Ailbe and 'placed her head on his bosom'. Ailbe remembered how he had been saved as an infant by wolves, so he promised that they would not be harmed. Instead, each day they came to Ailbe 'and ate with him, returning afterwards to their own places. And no one harmed them, and they harmed nobody.'

The Lives of Ailbe insist on an ecclesiastical pecking order. The opening statement of the Latin Life claims that he is 'bishop of the men of Munster, most blessed father, and second patron of the whole island after Patrick', despite the fact that Patrick 'came to Ireland later than Ailbe'. Another story in the Life describes how Ailbe took precedence over St Ibar. Ailbe too is said to have studied in Rome, with a bishop Hilary (who or may not have been a real historical figure). As well as Emly, he is associated with the church at Kilroot on the shores of Belfast Lough. The *Annals of Tigernach* gives three dates for his death (525, 532 and 541) and the *Annals of Inisfallen*, which draws on records originally compiled at Emly, says 528. However, these annals are not a contemporary record at this early date, and it is unlikely that he lived to such a late date if his mission had preceded the work of Patrick. His feast day is 12 September.

Despite these separate 'biographical' traditions, there is a strong possibility that St Abbán and St Ailbe, discussed above, were really the same person. Abbán is also a hypocoristic or pet name form of Ailbe. Pádraig Ó Riain argues that 'both linguistic and contextual evidence ... support the thesis that Ailbe and Abbán were one in origin.'

St Declan is associated with Ardmore on the coast of County Waterford, and is said to have founded the famous monastery there. A very fine collection of ecclesiastical remains survive at Ardmore to the present day, although the ruins which we can see almost certainly all date to a much later period than the time of St Declan. A stone-lined pit known traditionally as the saint's burial place can be found in the floor of the building known as St Declan's House or St Declan's Tomb, and there is a range of other features close by, such as St Declan's Well, associated in tradition with the saint.

Round towers are characteristic features of ancient Irish monasteries. One of the finest of them, dating to the twelfth century, stands near to the late twelfth-century St Declan's Cathedral. Inside this church can be found two stones with Ogham inscriptions, which must be among the earliest features on the site. Ogham is the oldest form of writing in Ireland and probably dates to the last few centuries before the introduction of Christianity or possibly to around the time to which we can assign St Declan himself, the fifth century. At that time Ardmore was in the territory of the people known as the Déisi. An old saying about him says: 'Let Declan be the Patrick of the Déisi, let the Déisi be with Declan forever.'

Lives of Declan survive in both Irish and Latin versions, the former probably merely a translation of the latter. Declan's father is said to have been chief of the Déisi, descended from ancestors who were kings of Tara, traditionally claimed as kings of all Ireland. Tara, County Meath, is located in lands which allegedly were originally held by the Déisi, but an old saga, subsequently incorporated into the Life of Declan, describes 'The Expulsion of the Déisi' and their journey to Munster.

The Life contains a story which seeks to explain how Declan's mission predated that of Patrick, while simultaneously acknowledging the authority of the latter. Declan is said to have studied in Rome, to have been ordained by the pope and then sent back to Ireland. On the return journey he met St Patrick, 'later sent by Pope Celestine to preach to the Irish'. The two clerics greeted each other and 'entered into mutual brotherhood'. Declan then came back to Ireland, ahead of Patrick. The Life further claims that while there were 'saintly bishops who were in Ireland with their disciples before Patrick ... it was St Patrick who converted most [and the most important] of the people of Ireland to the faith.'

St Declan's feast day is 24 July and on that day an annual 'round' or pilgrimage is held around the various monuments at Ardmore. In the past this was a major event in the local calendar, attracting large crowds from all over the province of Munster.

3. St Patrick and his Associates

St Patrick occupies a tremendously important place in Irish history and culture, for a number of reasons. In fact, the two texts he left behind, usually known as his *Confession* and the *Letter to Coroticus*, are the oldest in Irish history. The similar opening words of both works – in the *Confession*: 'I am Patrick, a sinner, the most unlearned of men, the least of all the faithful' – ring across the centuries, the first authentic voice of an individual in our long history.

Although various origins have been suggested for him, Patrick was almost certainly born in late Roman Britain, at a still positively unidentified place called *Bannaven Taberniae*, which was presumably somewhere near the western coast. His family were minor Christian nobles. Although neither of his writings is autobiographical in the modern sense, he does tell us that his father was a deacon called Calpornius, who was son of a priest, Potitus. At about fifteen years of age, Patrick (Patricius) was captured by Irish raiders and, along with others, brought to Ireland as a slave. Although later legends place his captivity at Slemish in County Antrim, modern scholars think that it is more probable that this period of his life was spent near the 'Wood of Voclut', the only place name he actually mentions in his writings. This is likely to have been on the northern coast of County Mayo, near present-day Killala and the significantly named Downpatrick Head.

After six years in Ireland he escaped and, following a number of adventures, got back safely to his home. He subsequently followed the example of his father and grandfather by becoming a cleric and, eventually, was made a bishop. In a dream he received letters headed

'The Voice of the Irish', which appealed to him 'to come and walk once more among us'. He returned to Ireland to preach the faith to the Irish pagans living at 'the ends of the earth'.

Although the Patrician legends would have it that Patrick single-handedly converted all of the Irish to Christianity, as we have seen, there are alternative claims from the south of the country. Patrick's work was almost certainly in the northern half of Ireland. In 431, Pope Celestine had sent the bishop Palladius 'to the Irish who believe in Christ', and other evidence suggests that Christianity had been filtering into Ireland from Roman Britain and Gaul for some time. Despite efforts by later supporters of Patrick to play down the achievements of Palladius, it is likely that his mission had some success, probably in Leinster.

Various dates have been proposed for Patrick's mission in Ireland, of which the best known are 432 for his arrival here and 461 for his death. An alternative date for his death is given in the *Annals of Tigernach* at 491, and scholars have tended to favour this later date. However, Oxford scholar David Howlett has recently argued that Patrick was born about 390, captured and brought to Ireland about 405 and escaped about 411, and that the dates for his return to Ireland in 432 and his death in 461 are probably correct.

Patrick is credited in later tradition as being the founder of the church of Armagh. In the following centuries, Armagh was promoted as the See of Patrick and hence the primatial church of the Irish. A number of texts were written, including several Lives of Patrick, which argue for and support this claim. On a secular, political level, the claim was also supported by the great royal Uí Néill dynasty, which, for much of the period from before AD500 to 1,000, provided some of the most powerful kings in Ireland. The Life of Patrick by Muirchú, probably written in the 690s, in a wonderful set-piece fictional story, brings Patrick to Tara to confront the early Uí Néill king, Laoghaire. Patrick was said to have lit the Paschal fire (symbol of Christianity) on the nearby Hill of Slane and the king's druid's advised that unless it was extinguished that night 'it will not be put out for ever'. Patrick then has to compete with the king's pagan druids, but bests them and, hence, secures the conversion of the king and his followers.

Another work, by Tírechán, probably written a decade or so before Muirchú's Life, brings Patrick on a journey around the northern half of Ireland, listing the churches founded (or claimed to have been founded) by him. Two very famous sites which later became attached to the cult of Patrick are St Patrick's Purgatory, an island on Lough Derg in County Donegal where people continue to go on retreat, and Croagh Patrick in County Mayo. Lough Derg had its own founding saint, **Dabheóg**, said to have been a Briton but of whom little else is known. His feast day is 1 January. The earliest historical evidence for St Patrick's Purgatory as a pilgrimage destination dates to the twelfth century. Throughout the middle ages the fame of the holy lake spread widely in Europe, generating its own literature as aristocratic and clerical visitors from the continent left descriptions of their otherworldly experiences there. Many of the beautiful, small, carved wooden 'Penal Crosses' are said originally to have been souvenirs of the pilgrimage to Lough Derg in the eighteenth and nineteenth centuries.

The practices associated with the annual climbing of Croagh Patrick (*Cruach Phádraig*, but known locally as the 'Reek') on the last Sunday in July would link it with the ancient festival of Lughnasa, around 1 August, in honour of the pre-Christian god Lugh. This is still one of the most important traditional pilgrimages in Ireland – if anything its popularity is growing – and in the past various 'pilgrims' ways' led from different directions towards this, the 'holiest' of Ireland's mountains. Some people still climb to the top – 750 metres (2,510 ft) –in their bare feet, praying and making the circuits of the various 'holy stations' along the route. St Patrick is said in legend to have fasted on this mountaintop for forty days and forty nights, and it was from here that he is also said to have driven the snakes out of Ireland.

> Holy Patrick, so full of grace,
> Suffered on Cruach, that blessed place,
> In grief and gloom enduring then
> For Ireland's women, Ireland's men.

Whatever about its pagan past, recent excavations have uncovered the remains of an early Christian oratory on the summit of Croagh Patrick. The structure, which is likely to have been similar to Gallarus oratory in County Kerry, has been dated by radiocarbon to between AD568 and 770.

Many other places in Ireland are associated with St Patrick, each with its own ancient legend. However, the well-known story of the saint using the shamrock to explain the mysteries of the Holy Trinity is not attested to in writing prior to the eighteenth century, although of course it could have been in oral circulation for a much longer period. As for the story of the snakes – there never have been any snakes native to Ireland.

A host of legends grew up around the story of Patrick and the historical Romanised cleric was soon given a very Celtic character. For example, the prayer or hymn known as 'St Patrick's Breastplate' is probably in origin a druidic spell, only thinly disguised:

I arise today
Through the strength of heaven:
Light of sun,
Radiance of moon,
Splendour of fire,
Speed of lightning,
Swiftness of wind,
Depth of sea,
Stability of earth
Firmness of rock ...
Christ to shield me today
Against poison, against burning,
Against drowning, against wounding ...

(trans: Kuno Meyer)

The various contradictions inherent in the early sources about St Patrick have confounded historians for a long time. Famously, in a celebrated lecture in 1942, TF O'Rahilly attempted to resolve these problems by proposing that there had been, in fact, 'two Patricks'. O'Rahilly's lecture at the Dublin Institute of Advanced Studies coincided with the publication of an agnostic scientific study by one of the Institute's other scholars. The *Irish Times* satirical columnist Myles na Gopaleen couldn't resist the opportunity to point out that it was only in Ireland that in the same year and in the same academic institution it could be proven that if there was no God, as compensation at least, there were two St Patricks!

As almost everyone in the world must be aware, St Patrick's feast day occurs on 17 March, a day now celebrated in the secular sense all over the world by the Irish or those who want to be associated with Ireland. This practice seems to have started with Irish exiles in continental Europe in the eighteenth century and to have spread from there to America and beyond.

The *Annals of Ulster* states that, in the year 439 (not a very reliable date), 'Secundinus, Auxilius and Iserninus, themselves bishops, are sent to Ireland to assist Patrick.' Not very much is known about this trio, but they are remembered as saints. The names of Auxilius and Iserninus are joined with that of Patrick on the so-called *First Synod of Patrick*, a very early set of church rules. The death of **Auxilius** (feast day 19 March), who is associated with the church of *Cell-Usailli* (Killashee near Naas, County Kildare), is given at 459 and that of **Iserninus** (who was known in Irish as Fith) at 468. The foundation of the churches at Kilcullen in Kildare and Ahade in Carlow is credited to Iserninus.

The death of **Secundinus** (known in Irish as Sechnall; feast day 27 November) in his seventy-fifth year is given in the annals at 447. He is said to have been the founder of the church of Dunshaughlin (*Domnach-Sechnaill*) in County Meath, and is credited with the composition of a Latin hymn, '*Audite Omnes*', in honour of St Patrick. Each new verse of the hymn starts with the next letter of the alphabet. In reality, the hymn probably dates to the early seventh century; the oldest version occurs in a manuscript known as the *Antiphonary of Bangor*, an early church service book dating to around the 680s. It is not possible to say with any certainty whether any of these clerics was really associated with Patrick; their missions in Ireland could have been quite separate.

A number of other saints, of whom little is known, are said to have been companions or disciples of Patrick. Among these, **Benignus** or Benén (feast day 9 November) is listed as Patrick's successor at Armagh. **Mochta**, the founder of the church of Louth, is described in the late seventh century as 'a British pilgrim ... a disciple of holy bishop Patrick'. His death is given in the annals at the year 535 and his feast day is 19 August.

In the Patrician legends, **Mac Cairthinn** was Patrick's 'strong man', carrying the saint on his back across rivers and on difficult pathways. As a reward he was given the church of Clogher, in County Tyrone, where there is also a complex of ancient 'royal' earthwork monuments dating to the Iron Age and later. Mac Cairthinn died, according to the annals, in 506. His feast day is 15 August. Like some of the other saints mentioned above, Mac Cairthinn's name links him with another of the 'sacred' trees of the Celts. Mac Cairthinn means something along the lines of 'devotee of the rowan tree'. The rowan tree or mountain ash was one of the most magical of trees for the ancient Irish.

4. St Brigid and her Associates

In medieval times, **St Brigid** (also Brigit, Bride, and so on) of Kildare was reckoned as one of the three 'patron' saints of Ireland. By the seventh century, the monastery of Kildare was a significant ecclesiastical centre, with communities of both men and women located there. Unusually, this monastery was under the governance of a woman, the abbess. Clearly this church, which had many specifically feminine attributes, had to have been founded by someone – possibly by a woman called Brigid. However, it is also clear that virtually no facts are known about this person and that the stories about St Brigid are heavily influenced by early mythology.

The site of the monastery at Kildare (*Cell Dara*, 'Church of the Oak'), itself seems to have had strong pre-Christian religious associations. The oak had a particular ritual significance for the pagan Celts, and we are told that the ancient tree from which the monastery was named was still living right up to the tenth century. Today there are few reminders of the sixth-century monastery. The medieval cathedral and its churchyard are probably on the original site. A plain high cross of the early Christian period can be found there, and nearby is the original monastic round tower, although this has lost its ancient conical cap.

Nearby are the remains of what is called St Brigid's Fire House, said to be the location of a sacred fire of ancient times. One of the daily duties of the nuns of Kildare was to look after this perpetual fire, which burned in the precincts of the monastery, a practice reminiscent of that of the Vestal Virgins of ancient Rome. In the late twelfth century, the Norman writer Gerald of Wales described this 'inextinguishable' fire:

It is not that it is strictly speaking inextinguishable, but that the nuns and holy women have so carefully and diligently kept and fed it with enough material, that through all the years from the time of the virgin saint until now it has never been extinguished. And although such an amount of wood over such a long time has been burned there, nevertheless the ashes have never increased.

Although in the time of Brigid there were twenty servants of the Lord here, Brigid herself being the twentieth, only nineteen have ever been here after her death until now, and the number has never increased. They all, however, take their turns, one each night, in guarding the fire. When the twentieth night comes, the nineteenth nun puts logs beside the fire and says:

'Brigid, guard your fire. This is your night.'

And in this way the fire is left there, and in the morning the wood, as usual, has been burnt and the fire is still all right.

This fire is surrounded by a hedge which is circular and made of withies, which no male may cross. And if by chance one does dare to enter – and some rash people have at times tried it – he does not escape divine vengeance. Only women are allowed to blow the fire, and then not with the breath of their mouths, but only with bellows or winnowing forks.

(trans: John O'Meara)

Gerald goes on to tell us about a Norman man who crossed the hedge and subsequently went mad, and another man whose foot perished after he had put it across the hedge.

Another significant mythological association with St Brigid is that her feast day, 1 February, is the ancient pagan festival of *Imbolg*, one of the four principal turning points (or 'borders') of the Celtic year. *Imbolg* appears to have been a springtime festival, marking the end of the winter. It had obvious fertility implications, especially celebrating the lactation of ewes and the lambing season. As an extension of this, a special responsibility for the protection of farm animals and crops was attributed to St Brigid.

The distinguished historian James Kenny says in his *Sources for the Early History of Ireland: Vol I, Ecclesiastical*: 'Brigid is one of the Irish saints as to whose relationship with a pagan divinity there can be little doubt.' In fact Brigid was the name of a Celtic goddess whose cult was widespread in Europe. The various peoples and tribes around Europe called the Brigantes take their name from the same source. Kenny quotes an ancient Irish text, which describes a trio of goddesses called Brigid:

> Brigid, a learned woman, daughter of the Dagda [the great, father god of the pagan Irish]. That is Brigid woman of learning, a goddess whom poets worshipped. For her protecting care was very great and very wonderful. So they call her goddess of poets. Her sisters were Brigid woman of healing and Brigid woman of smithcraft, daughters of the Dagda, from whose names among all the Irish a goddess used to be called Brigid.

Another scholar, Whitley Stokes, in the preface to his book *Three Irish Homilies*, summed up many of the mythological and liminal associations of St Brigid when he said that she:

> ... was born at sunrise [i.e. neither day nor night] neither within nor without a house [at the threshold], was bathed in milk, her breath revives the dead, a house in which she is staying flames up to heaven, cow-dung blazes before her ... she is fed from the milk of a white, red-eared cow; a fiery pillar rises over her head; sun rays support her wet cloak.

Despite these questionable aspects, Dr Daniel McCarthy has recently shown that the entry in the *Annals of Tigernach* for the birth (*nativitas*) of Brigid in 439 seems to be reliable, as is the entry recording her death in 524. According to one version of her life, she belonged to a people called the

Fotharta, who lived in western Leinster. In fact, a significant moment in the development of Brigid's cult seems to have been in 633, when Faolán mac Colmáin became king of Leinster. Faolán, whose brother was bishop of Kildare, was married to a woman who belonged to the Fotharta. It seems very probable that these coincidences resulted in the significant extension of Brigid's cult. However, another tradition places her birth at a place similarly called Faughart, now in County Louth, on the border of Ulster. In his book *Saint Patrick's World*, Liam de Paor points to the suitability of the latter place for a saint so involved with borders and turning points, both in space and time.

The Lives tell us that Brigid 'received the veil' (i.e. became a nun) at the hands of **St Mac Caille**, better known as St Mel, the patron of the diocese of Ardagh in Longford, whose feast day is 6 February. He, or another person of the same name, was believed to have been the nephew of St Patrick – a son of Patrick's sister, St Darerca. However there is no reliable historical evidence for any of this. A **St Darerca** associated with Valentia Island is called a sister of St Patrick. Her feast day is 22 March, but her relationship with the national apostle is almost certainly fictitious. There are, in fact, several other Darercas who were also venerated as saints.

After becoming a nun, Brigid is said to have gone on to found the monastery at Kildare. To celebrate the sacred liturgies and solemnities, a bishop (later to be known as **St Conlaed**, died 519) joined the community. When they died, both Conlaed's and Brigid's bodies were laid 'right and left of the ornamental altar [of the church at Kildare] placed in shrines decorated with a variegation of gold, silver, gems and precious stones, with gold and silver crowns hanging above them.' St Conlaed's feast day is 3 May. Conlaed is said to have ordained **St Tigernach**, the founder of the church of Clones, County Monaghan. Tigernach's father was from

Leinster but his mother belonged to the Airgialla, in whose territory Clones was located. Tigernach was bishop of Clogher, County Tyrone, also in Airgialla. His death is recorded at 544, and his feast day is 4 April.

Sometime around 680, a monk whose Christian name is known to us in its Latin form, Cogitosus, wrote a Life of St Brigid. He tells us that he had been pressed to do so by his brother monks. They almost certainly lived in the monastery at Kildare with which, it is clear from his text, Cogitosus is very familiar. Not much is known about Cogitosus. He belonged, he tells us, to the 'descendants of Aed', although who these people were we cannot say. Muirchú, the 'biographer' of St Patrick, tells us that Cogitosus was his spiritual 'father', probably in the sense that he provided a literary model for the former's writing about St Patrick. The feast day of a **St Cogitosus** is listed in the Irish martyrologies on 18 April, but this need not be the same person.

Despite the fact that Cogitosus tells us that an 'extensive tradition' about St Brigid had been 'passed down by people who are greater and more learned than I am', it is clear that he has very little real information about his subject. The Life is a succession of miracle stories some of which, even in the context of such a 'fabulous' genre, are fairly surprising. In one instance Brigid is out pasturing sheep. Her clothes are soaked by the rain, and when she returns home she hangs them to dry on a sunbeam.

Many of the miracles associated with this saint involve animals or food and drink. For instance, once while Brigid was travelling in the kingdom of Brega (now in County Meath), darkness came upon her and she had to spend the night with a poor old woman. The woman didn't have any wood to light a fire for her guest, so she broke up her precious weaving loom to use as fuel. Neither did she have much food, but she killed the only calf she had for her holy visitor. However, when they woke up the following morning, she 'discovered another calf, exactly the same as the calf she previously loved. And a loom was also found, exactly in the same shape and form as the one she had burned.' Brigid had worked the miracles in gratitude to the old woman. A later poem in Irish found in a manuscript now in the Royal Library in Brussels, whose words are put in the mouth of Brigid, continues this theme of hospitality:

> I should like a great lake of ale
> For the King of Kings;
> I should like the family of Heaven
> To be drinking it through time eternal.
> I should like the viands
> Of belief and pure piety;
> I should like flails
> Of penance at my house ...
> I should like vessels
> Of charity for distribution
> I should like caves
> Of mercy for their company
> I should like cheerfulness
> To be in their drinking;
> I should like Jesus
> To be here among them.

> *(trans: Eugene O'Curry)*

One very surprising miracle – some have described it as naive – tells how the saint terminates a pregnancy:

> A certain woman who had taken the vow of chastity fell, through youthful desire of pleasure, and her womb swelled with child. Brigid exercising the most potent strength of her ineffable faith, blessed her, causing the foetus to disappear, without coming to birth, and without pain. She faithfully returned the woman to health and to penance.

> *(trans: Liam de Paor)*

Like many of the Lives of the saints, this work is more valuable for throwing light on the period in which it was written than on the actual life of its subject. For example, Cogitosus's Life tells us quite a lot about the physical details of the monastery of Kildare in the late seventh century and, incidentally, about a number of contemporary issues, as diverse as road building and milling. Cogitosus describes the church of the monastery as:

> ... spacious in its floor area, and it rises to an extreme height. It is adorned with painted boards and has on the inside three wide chapels, all under the roof of the large building and separated by wooden partitions. One partition, which is decorated with painted images and is covered with linen, stretches transversely in the eastern part of the church ...
>
> *(trans: Liam de Paor)*

Although the Life has many peculiarities from a modern perspective, it is clear that it was written for the purpose of edification and to inculcate some important religious lessons. It has been argued that the Life stresses the important Christian virtues of faith, charity and virginity, even if the setting is a little unusual, such as in the story above about the pregnant woman.

Various additional Lives and other texts were written about her later. She is called: Prophetess of Christ, Queen of the South, Mary of the Gael. A beautiful hymn to her in Irish describes her as *Lóchrann geal na Laighneach/A' soilsiú feadh na tíre* – 'Shining lamp of Leinster/Lighting all the land'.

Notwithstanding the mixture of mythology and folklore which became incorporated in the legends about her, or perhaps even because of it, Brigid's popularity as a saint among the Irish was second only to that of Patrick. Many traditions about Brigid have survived down to our times.

Among these is the practice around her feast day of making St Brigid's crosses, distinctively shaped and made from rushes or straw.

St Brigid of Kildare, whether or not she really existed, should not be confused with the genuinely historical, fourteenth-century St Bridget of Sweden.

5. Other Women Saints

Ancient literature, as well as local traditions, includes the names of many women saints of whom little, other than their names, is known. For example, there are several saints listed in the martyrologies with the name Lasra or Lasar. These may actually all represent the same person or even some kind of pre-Christian deity, as the name seems to mean something like 'light' or 'burn'. However, real historical women were very active in the church in early Ireland, even if we know little about them. Kathleen Hughes points out in her book *Early Christian Ireland: Introduction to the Sources* that about 120 'women saints or groups of women are mentioned in the Martyrology of Tallaght ... yet we have Lives of only four'.

On the other hand, Liam de Paor draws attention to the fact that, while there is no real evidence for monasteries founded by males before about 535, at least some of the traditions associated with monasteries established by females do seem to date to a slightly earlier period – for example, 'St Brigid's' monastery at Kildare. De Paor goes on to point to the irony that it may have been communities of women who pioneered the great monastic movement, which was to be so influential in the Irish church from the sixth to the twelfth century. As another example, de Paor instances the case of **St Darerca** of Killeevy, who was also known as Moninna, and also, it appears, as Sarbhile.

Darerca appears to belong to the very earliest period of Christianity in Ireland. One (unreliable) tradition claims that she died in 518. The various Lives do, however, bring her into association with the earliest group of saints: Patrick, Brigid and, most interestingly, the pre-Patrician St Ibar. Darerca appears to have been her real name but, as mentioned above, she was also known by the hypocoristic or pet name Moninna. A legend explains that she got that name after she had cured a dumb poet, whose first words were 'Ninna, Ninna', hence Moninna or 'my Ninna'. Interestingly, because of this name, her cult became mixed up with that of St Modwenna, the patron of Burton-on-Trent in England. It is because of that confusion that we owe the survival in Burton-on-Trent of the bulk of the information about her.

She is said to have been born and reared in the County Down/County Louth area. It is claimed that her father was called Mocteus or Mochta. This is also the name of the early Louth saint mentioned above, an associate of St Patrick, and it may be that a tradition about Darerca's 'spiritual father' has become confused. St Patrick is credited with baptising her and commencing her instruction in Christianity.

As she could find no convent of nuns in her own territory, together with her companions Darerca crossed the country to the 'western islands', where St Ibar was at the time. Later she followed Ibar to Wexford but, on the way, stopped with St Brigid in Kildare. Again she set out for the north, stopping once more with St Brigid and founding a monastery near an unidentified place called *Ceann Trá*. Later she moved again, this time to County Louth where she lived at Faughart, the reputed place of St Brigid's birth, and where 'she never looked at a man'. Once again she moved; this time to the slope of Sliabh Gullion in County Armagh, where she founded her main monastery *Cell Sléibhe Cuillinn*, 'the church of Sliabh Gullion' or Killeevy. From there she sent a young novice, perhaps significantly called Brignat, to the great British monastery at Whithorn in Galloway. After many other miracles, the Life says she died on 6 July (her feast day) but went on working miracles even in death.

Her relics were kept at Killeevy: 'the hoe she used for digging ... her badger-skin garment ... and the wooden comb with which, once a year on the Feast of the Lord [possibly Christmas], it was her custom to comb her hair.' She herself, before she died, promised the local king that 'if you carry these [relics] with you against enemies who come to plunder your territories, God will grant you, through them, to be victorious.' This is reminiscent of later practices which we know about from historical documents, such as the carrying of the relics of St Colum Cille – the *Cathach* in Donegal and the *Brechbennoch* in Scotland – into battle.

St Moninna's feast day is 6 July. A site marked by a large granite slab at Killeevy, pointed out as her grave, and a nearby holy well are still visited by pilgrims on that day. The well is known as St Bline's Well, Bline being a local corruption of Moninna's name which is still used locally. As we would expect, nothing survives above ground dating to Moninna's own time. The ruins of two churches are preserved at the site – one is from the fifteenth century, but parts of the other may date back to the tenth century. We know that there was a round tower here also, but it fell down in the eighteenth century. The feminine aspect of this monastery was continued – as late as 1542 there was a convent of Augustinian nuns here.

St Íde or Ita, also known as Mida (from *Mo Íde*, 'my Íde', the hypocoristic or pet form of her name), as well as a number of other variants, was the foundress of a women's monastery at *Cluain Credail*, which translates as something like 'Holy Meadow'. This was Killeedy or *Cell Íta*, 'Ita's Church', at the foot of Sliabh Luachra near Newcastle West, County

Limerick. Íde is said to have had a school for little boys there. This gave her a reputation as the 'Foster Mother of the Irish Saints'. One of her pupils is said to have been St Brendan of Clonfert – Brendan the 'Navigator' – whom she advised to set sail in a wooden boat, 'as no boat for which blood had been spilled [i.e. a currach-type skin boat] could find the new world'.

Not very much is known in reality about Íde. She had another name – Deirdre. It is claimed that she was born about the turn of the fifth century and was of aristocratic blood, belonging, perhaps, to the Déisi of Waterford. An entry in the *Annals of Ulster* for 552 says that a local battle was gained 'through the prayers of Íde of Cluain Credail'. Her name is commemorated at Rosmead in County Westmeath and in a number of places in Cornwall.

One of the oddest stories told about Íde is how for a long time she endured a huge beetle eating away the side of her body. Her nuns killed the beetle, but Íde was very displeased. She said that the beetle was another of her fosterlings. Christ was pleased with this and so visited Íde in the form of a baby. This was said to be the occasion for the composition of the famous early Irish poem 'Ísucán', 'Little Jesus', attributed to Íde.

> ... Noble Jesus, angel-like
> A common cleric, not he.
> I nurse him at my desert place
> Jesus, the Hebrew baby ...

Íde's death is recorded in the *Annals of Tigernach* at 569; her feast day is 15 January. The monastery of Killeedy was probably turned over to men at some stage, as there are a number of references to abbots there at a later date.

St Attracta or Athracht is said to have founded a monastery at Killaracht, Coolavin, County Sligo, having taken the veil from St Patrick. A number of churches and places in the area are dedicated to her. Little is known about her, except for a tradition that she cared for the sick, and that her convent became a hospital. There is a Life of St Attracta of *Cell Saile* (in Crich Conaill, near Dundalk), who is probably the same saint. We have no dates for her life, but her feast day is celebrated on 9 February.

A very attractive female saint in terms of the stories told in folklore about her is **St Gobnat** of Ballyvourney, County Cork. However, there are few historical sources for her life. It is said that she was born in County Clare, and went to the Aran Islands to study with St Enda. There is a church dedicated to Gobnat on Inis Iar. An angel told her, however, that this would not be the 'place of her resurrection' (her death) and that she was to search Ireland until she found nine white deer, and there she should establish her main monastery. She set out, founding churches along her route, for example, at Dunquin in County Kerry and Dungarvan in County Waterford. Eventually she arrived in County Cork and, at different places, saw successively: three white deer, six white deer and nine white deer. At this last place she founded her monastery – this was Ballyvourney. Gobnat is remembered as caring for the sick. She is also a patron of bees. She used honey as a cure and, on one occasion, sent a swarm of bees to chase after a man who had stolen cattle. The cattle of course were returned. There are many other tales and legends about her, and her feast day is 11 February.

There is a **St Damhnat** associated with the monastery of Tedavnat (*Tech Damhnait*, 'Damhnat's House') in County Monaghan. Very little is known about Damhnat, but one of her feast days is 15 May. This coincides with that of St Dympna of Gheel in Belgium, with whom she is often equated. The legend of Dympna claims that she was the daughter of an Irish aristocrat who had a perverted sexual interest in her. She fled abroad and ended up in Gheel, to where she was pursued by her father. When she refused to return with him, he slew her. Hence she was venerated as a martyr. Apart from the unreliability of the legend itself, there are really no historical grounds for equating Damhnat and Dympna. The intercession of Dympna was credited with the healing of various disorders, especially mental illnesses. As a result of this she became venerated as the patron of the insane.

St Samthann was the patroness of the monastery of Clonbroney, near Granard in County Longford. Unlike the other saints mentioned, Samhthann was not the original foundress. One of the traditions of the monastery of Clonbroney claimed that it had been founded by St Patrick, but it was also claimed that it had been founded by followers of Brigid. Samthann was also believed to have been the abbess of a monastery at Urney, near Strabane in County Tyrone. Interestingly, Samthann is reputed to have been a lover of poetry or a poet. Her death is recorded in the *Annals of Ulster* in 739 and her feast day is 19 December.

6. The Two St Ciaráns

A number of St Ciaráns were commemorated in the Irish church. Two of these were very early saints who, occasionally, are confused with one another. The earliest of these is said to have been the 'elder', **St Ciarán of Saighir**. This Ciarán is claimed as another of the so-called pre-Patrician saints. In one of the Lives of St Ciarán it is claimed that 'before Patrick there were none to maintain faith and belief in Ireland but Ciarán, and Ailbe and Declan and bishop Ibar.' Ciarán comes so early in the sequence that we have no contemporary historical records of his life. All that we know about him comes from various Lives which were written down much later. Although these may to some extent reflect the actuality of what happened, they are clearly also charming works of fiction.

Ciarán's father belonged to the Osraige, who lived in what is now, roughly, the diocese of Ossory and County Kilkenny. On a trip to the southwest of Ireland he met a woman called Liadán, who belonged to the Corcu Loegde. These people lived in what is now, roughly, southwest Cork. Ciarán was born of their marriage and, according to the Lives, was fostered on Cape Clear, the southernmost point of Ireland. Ciarán is said to have spent thirty years on Cape Clear, praying and studying, but only 'what he received direct from heaven', as Christianity itself had not yet arrived in Ireland. There are still a number of monuments and features on Cape Clear dedicated to Ciarán, and 'rounds' or pilgrimages in his honour are still made on his feast days.

Ciarán set out for Rome, where he was baptized and where, for another thirty years, he studied the scripture and canon law 'under the abbot of Rome'. While journeying back towards

Ireland, Ciarán met St Patrick, who instructed him exactly where he was to go to found his monastery; at a place called Saighir. Thus, in this story there is a reconciliation of the apparent contradiction between St Patrick's primacy and the fact that Ciarán is still allowed to precede him as a missionary. A number of scholars have pointed out that the model of John the Baptist as the precursor of Jesus Christ seems to have been in the minds of the hagiographers when writing about Ciarán. Just like John the Baptist, Ciarán is portrayed as a wilderness figure; a friend of the wild animals. He himself was dressed in animal skins: 'these were the virtuous practices of Ciarán all his life; he never wore woollen clothes, but the skins of wolves and other brute beasts.'

At any rate, Ciarán returned to Ireland and came to Saighir (now Seirkieran, about four miles southeast of Birr, County Offaly). Saighir was to be the chief church of the Osraige for some time. Ciarán marked out the site for the monastery, but a wild boar approached and, cutting and rooting, tore down the trees, levelled the ground and dug the surrounding ditch for the saint. The boar also cut and dragged timber for Ciarán to build his hut. This boar was Ciarán's first monk. Then 'God gave additional monks to Ciarán ... a wolf with a badger and a fox in his train, and they remained with him doing him duty and service.' Ciarán's mother Liadán is said to have come to join him and to have founded a monastery nearby, specially for women.

The Lives then continue with the stock miracles told also about other saints. For instance, he can bring the dead back to life – he revives a lady called Eichill. He can travel to and return from great distances in one day. Like the Gospel miracle of the loaves and the fishes, Ciarán can feed a great crowd of people with 'seven oxen', and he blessed a well so that 'it had the taste of wine or honey for everyone who drank of it, so that the hosts [of people] were drunk as well as filled.'

Among these stories is one similar to that in the Life of Brigid, where he performs a miracle which terminates a pregnancy. In another parallel, we are told that a perpetual fire was kept at Saighir. The fire is given a Christian veneer, as we are told it was lit from Easter to Easter. Seirkieran is today a subcircular space of over ten acres surrounded by traces of the original monastic wall and ditch. A modern Protestant parish church marks the site, but there are also early church ruins and the foundations of a Round Tower, a number of early gravestones and the remains of a number of stone crosses. However very little if any of these features are likely to date back as far as Ciarán's time. We have no dates for the life of Ciarán but his feast day was celebrated on 5 March.

There is a Cornish saint known as St Piran or Perran. This seems to be the P-Celtic (British Celtic) form of the name Ciarán and it is clear that the written Life of Piran is simply an adaptation of the Life of Ciarán of Saighir. Scholars still argue as to whether there was a separate Cornish saint or whether the cult of Ciarán of Saighir had, simply, travelled to the other side of the Celtic Sea.

We are on slightly, but not massively, firmer ground when it comes to **St Ciarán of Clonmacnoise**. The *Annals of Tigernach* states that Ciarán was born in 514. Unlike other early saints, many of whom came from aristocratic back-grounds, Ciarán of Clonmacnoise is said to have come from very humble origins. He is often referred to in early litera-ture as *mac an tsaoir*, 'son of the wright' or 'son of the car-penter'. This association, together with the fact that he is said to have lived for thirty-three years, shows that his life

53

was paralleled with that of Jesus, in a somewhat similar way to the manner that Ciarán of Saighir was paralleled with John the Baptist. A number of Ciarán of Clonmacnoise's siblings were also said to be involved in the Church.

As a boy, Ciarán is said to have gone to study with St Finnian of Clonard, taking with him his dun cow. What was claimed as that cow's hide was to become one of the most famous relics in Ireland:

> That cow was dun [greyish-brown], and was called *Odhur Ciaráin*, and its fame remains forever in Ireland ... So its skin remains in honour even to this day in the monastery of St Ciarán; for through it, by the grace of God, miracles are performed. And above all it has this special virtue, as holy old men, the disciples of St Ciarán, have handed down to us, that it has been shown supernaturally that every man who shall have died resting on it, will possess eternal life with Christ.

Leabhar na hUidhre, the 'Book of the Dun Cow', one of Ireland's most important manuscripts, compiled in the twelfth century at Clonmacnoise, is said to have been written on this famous cow-skin. Whatever the truth, that is how the book got its name.

Following his stay at Clonard, Ciarán went to the other great Irish school of saints – St Enda's monastery, on Inishmore in the Aran Islands. By tradition, this was the earliest of the great Irish monasteries. **St Enda** (feast day 21 March), another very early saint, is said to have been persuaded by his sister **Fainche** (feast day 1 January) to become a monk. Significantly, Enda's tradition says that he studied monasticism in Britain and, in turn, many of the Irish monastic founders are said to have studied with him.

Ciarán is said to have been ordained by Enda and after that to have visited the monastery of **St Senán** (feast day 8 March), on Scattery Island in the mouth of the River

Shannon. Senán is another very early saint whose cult has many pre-Christian mythological associations. His name is tautological, possibly meaning something like 'Old Young', and his island monastery seems to have been the home previously of a 'monster' known as Catach. St Senán's Robe, the *Cassal Senáin*, is later said to have been one of the important relics preserved at Clonmacnoise in the early middle ages.

After his stay on Scattery Island, Ciarán continued his journey, following a stag, which led him to *Inis Ainghin*, Hare's Island in Lough Ree on the Shannon. Ciarán founded a monastery on that island and left his brother, **Donnán** (feast day 7 January), as abbot there. There is a more historical **St Donnán** who was martyred by sea pirates – possibly Vikings – in the year 616 on the island of Eigg, off the west Scottish coast, where he had established a monastery. The feast day of this Donnán is 17 April.

After Hare Island, Ciarán moved on downstream, finally arriving at a place then called *Ard Tiprat*, 'Height of the Well'. There he met Diarmait mac Cerball, great-grandson of the famous Niall of the Nine Hostages and a future high king of Tara. Diarmait was in hiding from the then king of Tara and helped Ciarán and his followers to establish a monastery. This incident is said to be depicted on the ninth- or tenth-century Cross of the Scriptures at Clonmacnoise. According to the *Annals of Ulster*, the year was 548, but the *Annals of Tigernach* says that Ciarán and Diarmait died in 543. Diarmait's relations with other clerics were not as congenial as those with Ciarán. During his time as high king at Tara, **St Ruadán of Lorrha** (feast day 15 April) and St Brendan of Birr are said to have cursed Diarmait by 'ringing their bells, both large and small, so violently that they damaged the bells in ringing them'. They also declared that, 'Tara shall be deserted for many centuries.'

However, the assistance Diarmait gave to Ciarán was more lasting. Henceforth the place was called *Cluain-moccu-Nóis*, 'Meadow of the people of Nós', or Clonmacnoise, from the people who granted the land for the monastery. Whatever its precise origins, Clonmacnoise was to become one of the most important monasteries in Ireland, as is testified by the imposing remains which survive there to the present day. Although ruinous, Clonmacnoise can give a visitor a powerful impression of what an early Irish monastery was like. The remains are very impressive, especially when approached on a boat on the River Shannon, the way many of the early travellers and pilgrims would have come. Clonmacnoise was also the hub of an ancient road system which utilised glacial eskers (raised linear deposits of gravel) to cross over the boglands of the centre of Ireland.

Underwater excavations in the Shannon in 1996 uncovered the remains of a seventeen-foot-wide bridge made from oak beams, which crossed the river nearby. The bridge dated to the early ninth century, later than St Ciarán's time. The same is true of the various structures and monuments which are dotted around the subcircular monastic enclosure. These include the round tower, a number of churches, a very fine collection of early grave-slabs and, among the stone crosses, the marvellous work of art and devotion known now as the Cross of the Scriptures. These all date to the centuries after St Ciarán's life and work, but they testify to the reverence in which his memory was maintained and his legacy developed. Clonmacnoise eventually grew into a large township; when the Normans attacked it in 1179 they burned over 100 houses.

Among the stories told in the Life of Ciarán is one in which merchants from Gaul come with wine to Clonmacnoise; the story gives us an insight into how trade was conducted at this early date. Ciarán is said to have mortified his body a lot as a form of penance. Another story tells of a 'stone cap' that Ciarán wore on his head. This was later revered as one of the chief relics of Clonmacnoise. The Life claims that Ciarán lived at Clonmacnoise for only one year, and the *Annals of Tigernach* records both the foundation of the monastery and the saint's death in 543. His feast day is 9 September.

7. The Three St Finnians and St Finbarr

Irish tradition remembers as distinct persons several saints with the name Finnian, or some variation of that name. Two of these Finnians were particularly famous, as was the Cork saint with the related name, Finbarr. However, it is clear that there is a great deal of confusion in the sources regarding these individuals and at least two of them, if not all three, may have been in origin the same person.

The earliest of these saints is said to have been **St Finnian of Clonard** (Finnio moccu Telduib, as well as several other variations). We have no information as to when he was born, but the main period of his activity is suggested as having been in the second quarter of the sixth century. He is treated as the initiator of monasticism in Ireland, which he is said to have learned in Britain, and he is brought into contact with the famous early British saints Cadoc, David and Gildas. When he returned from Britain, he is said to have first founded the monastery at Aghowle in County Wicklow. Later, he is claimed to have founded the monastery of Clonard on the River Boyne, now in County Meath but at that time on the borders of the ancient kingdoms of Leinster and Mide.

Clonard – *Cluain Iráird*, 'Erard's Meadow' – became famous as a school for monks and most of the great monastic founders are said to have studied there. Finnian's pupils included the so-called 'twelve apostles of Ireland'. Although there are various different lists of the saints who made up this 'twelve', they normally include: St Brendan of Birr, St Brendan of Clonfert, St Cainnech, St Ciarán of Clonmacnoise, St Ciarán of Saighir, St Colmán of Terryglass, St Colum Cille, St Mobhí of Glasnevin, St Molaisse of Devenish and St Ruadán of Lorrha.

The Life of Finnian of Clonard shows that many churches in Leinster and a few in north Connacht, such as those in Tirerrill, County Sligo, were associated with his cult. Finnian is said to have died in the great plague that devastated Ireland in 549 or 550. His feast day was 12 December. Today the main road from Dublin to Galway and the west of Ireland passes close to the site of the monastery of Clonard. Despite the fact that it survived as a significant settlement right through the middle ages, becoming the centre of the diocese of Meath in the twelfth century, not a stone of the ancient ecclesiastical buildings survives above ground to remind us that at one time this was a place of major importance.

St Finnian of Movilla is also said to have studied in Britain, with St Ninian, at Whithorn in Galloway. From there he is supposed to have gone to Rome before returning to Ireland, where he is credited with introducing the new version of the Bible, standardised in Latin by St Jerome, known as the *Vulgate*. Finnian founded the church of Movilla (*Magh Bhile*, 'Plain of the Sacred Tree'), at the head of Strangford Lough, near Newtownards in County Down. Finnian belonged to the local ruling dynasty in that part of Ulster, the *Dál Fiatach*. Like Finnian of Clonard, his name has many variations. The *Annals of Ulster* places his death in 579, calling him a bishop. His feast day is 10 September.

Finnian of Movilla is sometimes identified with St Frediano (feast day 18 March), a bishop of Lucca in northern Tuscany, Italy. Frediano's existence seems certain, although whether he was the son of a king of Ulster, as was later claimed, is less certain. The identification with Finnian seems very unlikely, but it had the advantage of helping to preserve some additional stories about the Movilla saint.

Adomnán, in his Life of Columba/Colum Cille written around about AD700, tells us that the subject of his work studied sacred scriptures with a bishop variously called Finnbarr, Finnio or Uinniau. This individual is often claimed to be St Finnian of Movilla. The name Finnian is a pet name form of the three names listed above. Richard Sharpe, in his book *Adomnán of Iona: Life of St Columba*, points out that, amid all this confusion, we can be certain that a 'holy man named Uinniau was influential as a monastic teacher in Ireland about the middle of the sixth century' and that, chronologically, this person could be 'a very plausible teacher' of Colum Cille. The form of his name Uinniau is British rather than Irish in origin (the initial U or V would have been rendered as an F sound in Ireland) and, as we have seen, the stories about both Finnian of Clonard and Finnian of Movilla suggest that they spent some time, at least, studying in Britain.

Uinniau wrote a book that has come to be known as the *Penitential of Finnian,* which he wrote 'out of affection and in the interests of religion, overflowing with the waters of the Scriptures, in order that by all men all evil deeds might be destroyed.' The *Penitential,* which is the earliest surviving Irish text of its kind, is basically a list of sins coupled with the appropriate penance:

> If anyone has decided on a scandalous deed and plotted in his heart to strike or kill his neighbour, if the offender is a cleric, he shall do penance for half a year with an allowance of bread and water and for a whole year abstain from wine and meat, and thus he will be reconciled to the altar [of God]; but if he is a layman, he shall do penance for a period of seven days; since he is a man of this world, his guilt is lighter in this world and his reward less in the world to come.

(Trans: Ludwig Bieler)

This Uinniau also sought advice from the British St Gildas on matters of monastic discipline, as is reported by St Columbanus in a letter he wrote to Pope Gregory the Great.

There is also a St Finnian associated with Druim Finn (now Dromin), near Ardee, County Louth. Little is known about him but, in the Life of Colum Cille, it is this Finnian who gives the loan of a book, the copying of which later gives rise to major problems for Colum Cille, as we shall see in the next chapter. Finnian of Dromin is often identified with Finnian of Movilla, and they may in fact have been, originally, the same person.

St Finbarr, or Bairrfind ('fair-headed'), is the patron saint of Cork. Pádraig Ó Riain, the scholar who has done most research on this saint, believes that, despite the fact that he is given a very different pedigree in the Lives, Finbarr of Cork is an alias of Finnian of Movilla. Ó Riain has characterised this individual in the following way: He was probably born and reared about the beginning of the sixth century in one of the various Irish colonies along the west coast of Britain. As a young man he came to Ireland and, at Movilla, 'devoted himself to a life of monastic discipline and scholarship'. He gained a well-deserved reputation, compiling the penitential named after him. As a young man St Colum Cille went to study with this Finbarr, who by then was an old man. The year of his death is not known, but his cult became widespread, often associated with that of Colum Cille's. How it became established in Cork, where the character of St Finbarr emerged from it, is not known.

Notwithstanding the controversial views of this modern scholar, there is a very formidable ancient tradition that St Finbarr of Cork was a genuinely historical and distinct person. Several Lives of this saint were written, all of which have been edited and translated in recent years by Professor Ó Riain. According to these Lives, the saint's original name was Lóchán, but when he went as a young man to be tonsured as a monk for the first time, the man shaving his head said:

> 'The hair of this servant of God is beautiful.' Another responded: 'You have spoken well, because his name will be changed and he shall be called Finn-barr, that is beautiful hair, from the beautiful hair he offered to the sacrifice of God.' Whence he was later called Finbarr by some and Barra by others, Barra being thence generally said in the Irish language.

This Barra later founded a number of schools, one of which was at a lake then called Loch Irce. This extraordinarily beautiful place, near the source of the River Lee, is now known in commemoration of the founding saint as Gougane Barra (Gougane, from Irish *Guagán*, seems to mean something like 'little fissure').

> The sanctuary of Loch Irce,
> Where is a sweet-toned bell;
> As numerous as leaves upon a tree,
> Are the saints who round it dwell.

Later Barra travelled on down the Lee Valley, to near where the river enters the sea:

> Barra remained on then in that place until his death. And a great monastery grew up there in his honour which is called by the name of Cork. Many holy men were pupils of his there ...

The site of this monastery is probably where St Fin Barre's Cathedral stands today, near the centre of Cork city. The stump of a round tower was found at the site, as well as a number of fragments from a Romanesque building of around the twelfth century. Cork was Finbarr's most important church, but in one story St Brendan of Birr acknowledges that God had 'made subject to Barra for ever' the regions 'from the Blackwater to the Lee and from the Lee to the Bandon river and to Beara and from the Bandon river to Clear Island'. Despite Finbarr's attachment to Cork, that is not where he died. When his death drew near he went to Cloyne and 'yielded up his spirit to heaven' at a cross in the middle of that monastery.

> Afterwards his monks and disciples and the clergy of the churches of south Munster came to wake and honour the body of their master, holy Barra, and they removed it to the place of its resurrection in Cork.
>
> That day of holy Barra's death, moreover, was prolonged for the clergy. God did not allow the sun to descend below ground for twelve days ...

The feast day of St Finbarr of Cork is 25 September.

The stories about the various St Finnians, and the saints with similar names, provide us with an excellent example of the complexities of early Irish history and hagiography.

8. St Colum Cille

Unlike the other two patron saints of Ireland, Patrick and Brigid, we are on much surer historical ground when it comes to St Colum Cille (or Columba as he was known in Latin). About one hundred years after his death, his Life was written in Latin by his relative and successor Adomnán. Adomnán's text, together with other sources, can be used to reconstruct some of the details of his life and to separate out some of the welter of legends which grew up around this most popular of saints. Thanks to the work of Dr Daniel McCarthy, we can be fairly confident that Colum Cille was born in the year 520. Tradition says that he was born on the day that **St Buite**, the founder of the monastery of Monasterboice, died – 7 December (Buite's feast day). Several poems (as it happens retrospectively) claim that his birth was predicted.

> A boy will be born in the north,
> He will come after so many years;
> Ireland he'll set alight, and
> His death will leave Scotland in tears.

Colum Cille's family belonged to a local royal dynasty from what is now County Donegal. That dynasty, the Cenél Conaill, often provided incumbents for the overkingship of the great confederation of peoples known as the Uí Néill, who dominated the northern half of Ireland in the period roughly from AD500 to 1000. The high king of Tara for much of this time was the head of the Uí Néill. The incumbent of this office was not quite the king of Ireland, as has often been claimed in the past, but he was certainly one of the most powerful leaders in the country. Later legends claim that Colum Cille could himself have become high king, and it is

Right: A medieval wooden statue said to depict St Molaisse. Originally from Inishmurray, County Sligo, it is now housed in the National Museum of Ireland.

Below: Two cross-slabs on Inishmurray. The monastery on the island is said to have been founded by St Muiredach, and is associated with St Molaisse.

Above: Graveyard at St Mullins, the site of St Moling's monastery, by the River Barrow in County Carlow.
Below: Skellig Michael, off the coast of County Kerry, the remote location of an important early Christian hermitage.

Above: St Colum Cille in the oak grove of Derry – a stained-glass window in the Guild Hall, Derry.
Below: A page from the Cathach, a copy of the psalter, traditionally claimed to have been written by St Colum Cille.

Above: The cross-slab and church at Glencolumbkille, County Donegal, two of the 'stations' on the famous 'turas', or pilgrimage route, around the valley.
Below: Collecting water from the holy well at St Gobnait's Shrine, Ballyvourney, County Cork.

Above: The building known as St Colum Cille's House at Kells, County Meath. The monastery there was founded in the early ninth century and became one of the most important Columban foundations.

Above: The Cross of the Scriptures at Clonmacnoise, County Offaly. The lowest panel on the shaft is said to depict St Ciaran founding the monastery, being assisted by Diarmait mac Cerball.

Above: The round tower at Glendalough, County Wicklow, where St Kevin founded his monastery in the late sixth century.
Right: St Fin Barre's Cathedral, Cork city, on the site of the saint's monastery.

Above: Pilgrims climbing Croagh Patrick, County Mayo, Ireland's holiest mountain, from where St Patrick is said to have banished the snakes.

certainly true that he was extremely influential in the highest aristocratic circles, both in Ireland and northern Britain.

One tradition points to the exact spot, at Gartan in County Donegal, where Colum Cille is said to have been born. This is *Leac na Cumhadh*, the 'Stone of Sorrow/Loneliness'. In the nineteenth and early twentieth centuries it was the practice of many intending Donegal emigrants to spend the night before their departure from their homeland sleeping on this stone. It was believed that this practice would later assuage the pangs of homesickness they expected to suffer when they left Ireland. The belief was that by doing this, Colum Cille, himself an emigrant, would protect them in their new life. Tradition, which in some ways can be so precise, can also be very fickle, and another site at Churchtown, about a mile away from the celebrated stone, is also claimed as the birthplace of the saint. A *turas* or 'pilgrimage' is held here annually on the saint's feast day. Throughout the year, the little altar at the site is heaped with the trifle offerings of those who come to seek the assistance of the saint for their earthly requests.

Colum Cille's father was called Feidlimid (Felim or Phelim). He was said to be a great grandson of the legendary king Niall of the Nine Hostages, who commenced the Uí Néill dynasty.

> A son shall be born to Feidlimid,
> A jewel in every assembly field;
> Feidlimid the son of Fergus,
> The son of Conall son of Niall.

The saint had at least one brother, Iogen, and three sisters: Cuimne, Sinech and Mincoleth (mother of the sons of Enan – after whom Kilmacrennan in Donegal is named). Colum Cille's mother was called **Eithne**, and she too was later venerated as a saint. She is sometimes equated with the saint of that name whose feast day occurs on 26 February. The reputed site of Eithne's grave is situated on the island of Eileach an Naoimh, in the Garvellachs, south of Mull in the Scottish Inner Hebrides. Several other members of Colum Cille's close family became monks and priests, and some of these were also commemorated as minor saints.

Colum Cille's childhood is said to have been spent in the area around Kilmacrennan, the original name of which was *Doire Eithne*, the 'Oakwood of Eithne' (his mother's name). One legend about him tells us that the boy was originally called Crimthann, a name which means something like 'fox' or 'deceitful one'. However, the angels considered this to be an unsuitable name and inspired his companions to call him Colum Cille, 'Dove of the Church'. It is not certain that this name was ever used for him when he was alive. Although it occurs in very early texts about him, and the Latin name Columba (also meaning 'dove') was almost certainly his 'Christian' name, the full title Colum Cille may itself be part of the growth of his legend.

The Latin Life of Colum Cille tells us that while still a deacon, he spent some time in Leinster studying with an 'old master' called Gemmán. He is also said to have studied sacred scripture with a bishop Uinniau, sometimes identified with St Finbarr or with one of the SS Finnian (who might actually be the same person) discussed in the last chapter. Another tradition claims that he studied at the monastery of Glasnevin in Dublin, with **St Mobhí** (feast day 12 October). Although there are very many wonderful legends which purport to tell us about Colum Cille's life as a young cleric, the fact is that it is only with his departure for Iona in the year 562, when he was already about forty-two years of age, that we have any reliable information about his work as a founder of monasteries. He is credited with founding Derry – his first and therefore most beloved church – as early as

546 (according to the *Annals of Ulster*), but it is clear now that this is far too early a date, and the name of an alternative founder is also recorded in the annals. Many other monasteries in Ireland – such as Drumcliff in County Sligo, Moone in County Kildare and Swords in north County Dublin – were also claimed to have been founded by Colum Cille, but it is certain that they too were founded much later. One such place was Kells, now in County Meath, where the famous Book of Kells comes from. In fact this famous manuscript is sometimes attributed to the saint and was often called St Colum Cille's Gospel. The book was almost certainly made on the island of Iona about AD800. It has been suggested by some scholars that it might have been made as a memorial object for the second centenary of Colum Cille's death. Likewise, despite traditions which claim that the monastery of Kells was founded by the saint in the sixth century, we know that it was actually established at the beginning of the ninth century.

The one monastery that we can be certain that Colum Cille did found in Ireland was Durrow in County Offaly, probably in the 580s on one of his return trips from Iona. Other places which have strong traditional connections with the saint include the dramatic Tory island, nine miles off the coast of County Donegal, and the beautiful Glencolumbkille in the same county. At Glencolumbkille, a series of ancient monuments, mounds of stones and beautifully carved cross-slabs scattered around the valley have been incorporated into the *turas*, the traditional pilgrimage in honour of the saint. This pilgrimage can be made at any time of the year but most especially on the saint's feast day.

Adomnán vaguely links Colum Cille's departure from Ireland for Iona with the battle of Cúl Dreimne, which took place in the year 560. Cúl Dreimne is in the vicinity of Drumcliff, County Sligo, where there was later a monastery dedicated to St Colum Cille (incidentally, the graveyard which occupies part of the site of the monastery is where the poet WB Yeats is buried). The annals, in recording the Battle of Cúl Dreimne, say that victory was gained 'through the prayer of Colum Cille' for his own people, the northern section of the Uí Néill dynasty. They also add that the enemy, the southern section of the Uí Néill, had the benefit of an additional exotic weapon – a 'druidic fence' of some kind. The battle fought between these two sections of the Uí Néill was probably part of the normal dynastic politics of the Ireland of the time. For whatever reason, however, this battle was remembered as a sort of contest between the forces of Christianity on the one side and those of pagan druidism on the other. The true story of the battle became enshrouded in a number of legends which suggest that Colum Cille himself was to some extent responsible for it.

In these stories, Colum Cille is said to have copied a manuscript of the Psalms without the permission of its owner, St Finnian of Dromin. After it was made, St Finnian claimed that the copy as well as the original belonged to him. This, of course, very much angered Colum Cille, who had laboured hard to make the copy. The matter was referred to the high king at Tara, Diarmait mac Cerball. Diarmait delivered the famous judgement against Colum Cille: *Le gach boin a boinín, le gach leabhar a leabhrán,* 'To every cow its calf, to every book its copy'.

It is often claimed that this is one of the oldest references in history to the concept of copyright but, unfortunately, we now know that the story belongs to a much later date than the sixth century. At any rate, this judgement and a number of other insults by Diarmait are said to have so annoyed Colum Cille's people that they fought the battle against the high king and his people. In this

version of the story, Colum Cille's guilt at his own involve-
ment in the battle led to his going into exile as a penance.
Modern scholars, and the earliest sources available, would
suggest, however, that Colum Cille's exile was voluntary –
Adomnán called him a 'pilgrim for Christ'. This sort of practice, exile for the love of God, became known in the Irish
church as 'white martyrdom'.

Almost every aspect of Colum Cille's life became heavily
mythologised. One example of this was his departure from
Ireland. The medieval writers turned this into one of the
great tragedies of Irish history. Not only the people
lamented his going, but so did all of nature. His boat sailing
down Lough Foyle was said to have been followed by seagulls 'screaming and screeching for grief that Colum Cille
was leaving Ireland'. The fact that seagulls follow every boat
leaving every harbour hardly detracts from the appropriate-
ness of the literary image employed by the hagiographers.

Colum Cille eventually established his most important
monastery (probably in 562) on Iona, a small island off the
Isle of Mull, itself off the west coast of Scotland. This was to
become one of the most influential ecclesiastical centres in
Christendom.

Evidence from archaeological excavation shows that the
island had been inhabited in prehistoric times, but that it
was probably deserted when Colum Cille and his monks
arrived there. A rectangular earthwork enclosing about
eight acres of land, which had apparently been built by earlier settlers, was re-occupied by the Irish monks and within
it they built their monastery. Part of the enclosing bank still
survives, but there is little else visible on the surface which
dates from the sixth century. We can, however, get some
impression of what the original monastery was like from the
writings of Colum Cille's seventh-century relative and successor, Adomnán. The great restored Benedictine abbey

which now dominates the island was begun in the early thirteenth century. There are some earlier buildings, however, including one which is reputed to be the burial place of the saint, despite a tradition that says he was reburied at Downpatrick. Among the glories of the monastery of Iona are the three great High Crosses, dedicated respectively to St Oran, St John and St Martin. These seem to have been carved in that order between about AD750 and 800.

Many other churches and monasteries were founded from Iona; some of these, although not all the ones that were claimed, were founded within the lifetime of the saint. Colum Cille certainly did travel away from Iona, up the Great Glen of Scotland and even back to Ireland. We know that he attended a significant meeting in Ireland sometime around 590, between his relative, the important Donegal king Aed mac Ainmerech, and the king of an Irish colony in Scotland, Aedán mac Gabráin. The Convention of Drum Ceat, as this meeting came to be known, was held near Limavady in County Derry, and gave rise, itself, to a whole host of legends, among them the amusing story of the saint's footwear. Medieval writers, who had elaborated the legends in which Colum Cille swore that as a penance he would never set foot on Irish soil again, were forced to invent extraordinary explanations about how he kept this promise. For the Convention of Drum Ceat, Colum Cille attached two sods of Scottish turf to his feet and accordingly never did stand on Irish soil, just as he had vowed. Many such stories are told about this larger-than-life saint.

Colum Cille is remembered as the poet saint. A number of Latin poems said to have been composed by him are possibly genuine, but there are many others in Irish which later propagandist poets put in the mouth of the saint.

And oh! Were the tributes of Alba [Scotland] mine,
From shore unto centre, from centre to sea,
The site of one house, to be marked by a line,
In the midst of fair Derry were dearer to me.
That spot is the dearest on Erin's ground,
For its peace and its beauty I give it my love;
Each leaf of the oaks around Derry is found
To be crowded with angels from heaven above.
My Derry, my Derry, little oak grove,
My dwelling, my home, and my own little cell;
May god the Eternal, in heaven above,
Send woe to thy foes and defend thee well.

(trans: Douglas Hyde)

Continuing this theme of the poet saint, Colum Cille is said to have saved the pagan poets from expulsion from Ireland at the Convention of Drum Ceat. We know that he did write himself. The apparently contemporary – and oldest Irish – manuscript, a copy of the Psalms known as the *Cathach*, dating to about the end of the sixth century, is said to be his work. Such a claim hasn't been proven, but neither has it been disproved and it is just possible that our oldest manuscript, and one of our most beautiful, is written in the hand of one of our most interesting saints.

It used to be believed that Colum Cille had died in 597, on 9 June (his feast day), but recent research points to the year 593. Very shortly after his death, the long poem known as the '*Amra Colum Cille*' ('Eulogy of Colum Cille') was written by the famous poet Dallán Forgail. Other similar poems praising Colum Cille were written in the seventh century. We know also that a *Liber de Virtutibus Sancti Columbae* – 'Book on the Virtues of Saint Columba' – was compiled in the mid-seventh century, although only one paragraph from it survives, as a quotation in one of the versions of Adomnán's Life. In the later twelfth century, another Life of

Colum Cille was written in the Irish language. This Life, probably written in Derry, took the form of a homily or sermon for preaching on the saint's feast day. The text is structured largely as an account of the saint's journey around Ireland, founding churches and monasteries as he went.

But by far the most elaborate Life of Colum Cille is that written in 1532, just over a thousand years after his birth. This was composed by Manus O'Donnell, who, five years later, would become chieftain of Tír Conaill, or Donegal. Many other works have been written about Colum Cille, each of which developed the fabulous legends about him, creating ever more distance between the fictional character and the original sixth-century monk.

9. Colum Cille's Associates

Adomnán wrote his Life of Columba at the end of the seventh century. Some scholars have suggested that the occasion was the one-hundredth anniversary of his subject's death, in the 690s. The spirituality which he attributed in the Life to Colum Cille was obviously very close to Adomnán's own heart, and he too was honoured as a saint, with a feast day on 23 September.

A short poem in Irish – almost certainly later in date, but called 'The Prayer of St Adomnán' – is included in the tenth-century *Liber Hymnorum*:

> Colum Cille,
> To God, please commend me
> When the time comes to die.
> May it not come too soon ...

The *Annals of Tigernach* says that Adomnán was born in 625. It is claimed that he belonged to Colum Cille's own people, the Cenél Conaill of Donegal. Although there is no historical evidence to confirm it, Adomnán is credited with the foundation of the monastery of Raphoe in Donegal. He is still, under the anglicised name Eunan, the patron of the Diocese of Raphoe. Traditions associate him with the other Columban (i.e. associated with Colum Cille) churches of Durrow in County Offaly and Drumhome in County Donegal, but the first really firm evidence we have for his life is when he became ninth abbot of Iona in 679/680. He became a very influential ecclesiastic, both in Ireland and Britain; as well as the great authority he possessed in Scotland, he was also a friend of Aldfrith, king of Northumbria. According to the early English historian and saint, the Venerable Bede, this Aldfrith knew the Irish language, is said to have had an Irish mother and, himself, had an Irish name, Flann Fína.

Besides his *Vita Columbae,* Adomnán wrote a number of other works; among them *De Locis Sanctis.* This was a description of the shrines of the Holy Land, which Adomnán had obtained from a Gaulish bishop who had come to Iona. Among a number of other occasions, Adomnán returned to Ireland in 697, the year he believed to be one-hundredth anniversary of his predecessor's death. The main purpose of his visit was to lead the Synod of Birr (in County Offaly) and, as the annals say, to give 'the Law of Innocents to the people'. The Law of Innocents, or Adomnán's Law as it was also known, was designed to protect children, women and clerics from combat and to take them under the protective wing of Iona and the churches of Colum Cille. It has been described as an early form of the Geneva Convention. The synod which enacted it was attended by a host of the most senior clerics and lay men from both Ireland and Scotland, led by the King of Tara, Loingsech mac Oengusso, another of Adomnán's relatives. All these powerful people guaranteed to implement Adomnán's Law of Innocents. There could have been no greater tribute to the spiritual influence wielded by Adomnán in these islands.

Adomnán died on Iona in 704. By 727 when, according to the annals, his relics were brought 'to Ireland and the Law [of Innocents] was promulgated anew', Adomnán was clearly perceived as a saint. A Life of Adomnán in Irish survives, in the form of a sermon for preaching on his feast day. It was written, according to the scholars Máire Herbert and Pádraig Ó Riain, in the Columban monastery at Kells in County Meath between the years 956 and 964. Although it is possible that it contains some evidence of Adomnán's activities, the Life is largely a work of fiction, in effect a *roman-a-clef* in which the political events of the author's own lifetime are presented in terms of that of the saint's.

Iona was the mother church of many other monasteries founded in Scotland, Ireland and the north of England. One of these was the famous monastery of Lindisfarne, on Holy Island off the coast of Northumberland. This was established in 635 by the Irish monk who would become known as **St Aidan**, whose feast day occurs on 31 August. Lindisfarne was given to Aidan by King Oswald of Northumbria, who had spent some time on Iona. The Venerable Bede, who recorded a great deal about the influences stemming from Colum Cille's Iona, tells us that Oswald had learned to speak the Irish language while staying on Iona. Oswald was himself venerated as a saint of the English church, with a feast day on 9 August.

Another saint connected with Lindisfarne and Iona was **St Colmán** (feast day 18 February), who left England with some companions and returned to Ireland in 664, taking with him as relics pieces of his predecessor Aidan's bones. Colmán founded the monastery of Inishbofin, off the Galway coast, in 668, from which was later founded another separate monastery for English monks, at the village of Mayo on the mainland.

In 732 the *Annals of Ulster* records that 'the pontiff of Mayo of the Saxons, Gerald, died.' This is **St Gerald**, whose feast day is 13 March, although a Life of the saint associates him unhistorically with characters from an earlier age. In one fabulous story in the Life, the kings of Ireland held an assembly to discuss the problem of over-population in the country. It was proposed that God should be asked to send a plague to the 'lower orders' to solve the problem. **St Fechín** of Fore in County Westmeath is said to have supported the idea, using the time-honoured Irish method of applying pressure, by ritual fasting (or hunger striking) on God. The result was the plague of 664, in which Fechín and many other clerics died. In the story, of course, Gerald was saved.

Whatever about any such odd ideas, Fechín is credited with the foundation of churches at Ballysodare in Sligo, Termonfeckin (*Tearmon Fechín*, 'Fechín's refuge') in County Louth, Omey Island, High Island and Cong in Galway. This last church was the original home of the twelfth-century Cross of Cong, made as a shrine for what was believed to be a fragment of the True Cross. Fechín's feast day is 20 January.

The *Annals of Tigernach* reports the birth of **St Cainnech** of Aghaboe in 518, and his death in 598. His feast day is 11 October. Aghaboe or *Achad Bó,* 'The Cow Field', now in County Laois, was in the ancient territory of the Osraige, a people who lived in the border lands between Leinster and Munster. Their kingdom is best represented nowadays by the Diocese of Ossory or, roughly, by County Kilkenny. In fact, Kilkenny – *Cill Cainnigh*, 'Canice's Church' – takes its name from this sixth-century saint, who is also said to have founded the church there. St Canice's Cathedral, with its round tower, is probably located on the site of the original monastic church. Kilkenny only took over from Aghaboe as the chief church of the Osraige in the twelfth century.

Cainnech is also credited with founding the church of Clonbroney, near Birr in County Offaly. A Life of St

Cainnech in Latin, possibly written as early as the eighth century, survives, but even earlier evidence about him is contained in Adomnán's Life of Columba. According to his own Life, Cainnech was said to have been born in Ciannachta, nowadays near Limavady in County Derry. A nearby church, at Drumachose, is dedicated to him. He is said to have been fostered in Leinster and to have spent some time in Britain. Adomnán tells of him coming to Iona, and there are many dedications to him throughout Scotland where he is sometimes known by the anglicised name of Kenneth. The stories show St Cainnech to have been a friend of St Colum Cille, but could they have had a closer relationship?

Professor Pádraig Ó Riain, in a complicated but ingenious study published in 1983, argues that they are one and the same person. In other words, in some of the stories the character of Colum Cille has been split, as it were, into two distinct persons – himself and Cainnech. If this did happen, it had to have been well before Adomnán wrote his Life of Columba at the end of the seventh century as, in that work, Colum Cille and Cainnech are understood to be two quite distinct characters.

Ó Riain's argument is partially based on showing that Cainnech is a variation of the name Colum (technically a diminutive hypocoristic form, i.e. an endearing version of the basic name, meaning something like 'dear little Colum'). These endearing or 'pet' names, as we have already seen, were a popular feature of the earliest phase of Christianity in Ireland. Depending on what prefixes and endings were attached to the original, or 'radical', name, as well as some additional linguistic variations which might have depended on dialect or other local differences, a single name could be transformed into a whole host of variations. In fact, Ó Riain shows us that Caimme, Caimmíne, Cainne, Cainnech, Cainneóc, Cammán,

Cammóc, Coimme, Coinne, Colmán, Commae, Commán, Conna, Conóc, Cuimmíne, Cumma, Cummóc, Dochonna, Mocholmóc, Mochonna, Mochonóc, and Mochumma are all variations of the simple name Colum. In a period when communication would have been extremely difficult, it is easy to see how the same person, but referred to by different names in different parts of the country, could be split into a number of distinct characters.

One of the variations of the name Colum mentioned above is Colmán. In a list of saints in the twelfth-century *Book of Leinster*, not less than 228 saints bear the name Colmán. However, in the same study already referred to above, Ó Riain shows again that the apparently distinct **St Colmán** of Dromore is in reality also a variation of Colum Cille. Dromore, on the River Lagan, is now a village in County Down. Its ancient church, said to have been founded by St Colmán, also gave its name to the larger diocese. The feast day of St Colmán – who was also known as Mocholmóc, 'my little Colum' – is 7 June, significantly two days before that of Colum Cille. A Life of St Colmán in Latin survives, but has been dismissed by historians as 'short and fabulous'. It is little more than a set of stock miracle stories. For what it is worth, it tells us that Colmán studied with **St Caelán** (feast day 29 October) of Nendrum, a monastery on the shores of Strangford Lough where very significant remains are still visible.

Another saint with the same name is **St Colmán mac Duach**, whose main church was at Kilmacduagh, in the Burren (though actually in County Galway). This site has one of the best collections of medieval church buildings in Ireland, including the thirty-metre-high round tower, which tilts slightly. This St Colmán, whose feast day occurs on 3 February, is said to have founded two churches on Inishmore in the Aran Islands and another Burren church at Oughtmama. As if to strengthen the suggestion of a connection with the saint of Iona, there is a place called Glencolumcille nearby.

10. The Two Saint Brendans

For both the years 564 and 572, the *Annals of Tigernach* records the death of **St Brendan of Birr**. Not very much is known about him. But he was often described in ancient literature as 'the elder', in order to distinguish him from his near contemporary namesake. He is associated in hagiography with St Colum Cille – indeed, one story has it that it was Brendan who instructed Colum Cille to go to Iona. Another story, told by Adomnán in his Life of Columba, tells how the latter was excommunicated 'for some trivial and quite excusable offences'. Colum Cille went to the assembly of churchmen at Tailtiu (Teltown, County Meath) that had excommunicated him. As he approached the gathering, St Brendan, 'the founder of the monastery of Birr', rose to greet him and kissed him reverently. The senior clerics remonstrated with Brendan for acting respectfully towards the excommunicate. However, Brendan explained to the assembly that he had seen a vision surrounding Colum Cille, a sign that God really favoured this man. After this the charges against Colum Cille were dropped.

Another story tells of when Brendan was a student with St Ciarán at Clonard. A beautiful flower from the 'Land of Promise' appeared to the 'twelve apostles of Ireland', who were all studying there at the time. St Brendan of Birr was selected by his colleagues to go in search of that land but, because he was old, St Brendan of Clonfert was chosen to go in his place. There are some other allusions to sea voyages in various anecdotes told about Brendan of Birr, and it seems certain that there were at least some connections between the two Brendans. Brendan of Birr's feast day is 29 November. Although there are a number of fanciful explanations for it, the name Brendan is said to be a borrowing into Irish of *brenhin,* an ancient British (what we would call Welsh) word for a king.

Adomnán also tells a story about how, when visiting Iona, Brendan moccu Altae saw a vision surrounding St Colum Cille. This is **St Brendan of Clonfert**, 'Brendan the Navigator', although, as suggested above, it has been argued that the two Brendans are really one and the same person. Whether this is true or not, the sources tell us a lot more about this Brendan. He belonged to the ancient people called the Ciarraige, who were originally located in several places in the south and west of Ireland. One group of them, the Ciarraige Luachra, lived in what is now County Kerry, around Dingle in Tralee Bay. In fact, the county takes its name from these people. Brendan is said to have belonged to one of their important families. Many places in Kerry were named after him, such as Brandon Creek and Mount Brandon on the Dingle Peninsula, and there is still considerable devotion to him in Kerry. Many pilgrims climb to the summit of Mount Brandon in his honour, along the *Cosán na Naomh* or 'Saints' Path', especially on his feast day.

Brendan is said to have been fostered by St Íde at Killeedy and later, having been educated by a bishop Erc, to have become a monk and a priest. The *Annals of Tigernach* records the foundation of Clonfert (*Cluain Ferta Brenaind,* 'Brendan's meadow of graves' or 'Brendan's meadow of miracles') in 558. Clonfert is in County Galway, close to the Shannon and Lough Derg, and one of the finest Irish Romanesque churches in the country can be found there, dating from the twelfth-century. Other church sites, on islands in Lough Corrib and in the Shannon, are also said to have been founded by Brendan. His principal church in Kerry was at Ardfert (*Ard Ferta,* 'height of the graves/miracles'). He is also credited with founding a monastery at a place called *Ailech* in the Hebrides in Scotland. This is possibly *Eileach an Naoimh*, the traditional burial place of Colum Cille's mother Eithne. The unidentified church at *Bledach* on Tiree is also said to have been founded by Brendan. In addition, his cult spread to parts of Wales and Brittany.

Despite the fact that his chief church at Clonfert is inland, Brendan's cult is mainly found in coastal locations. He is the hero of a great sea-voyage tale written in Latin, the *Navigatio Brendani,* or 'Voyage of Brendan'. In ancient secular literature written in Irish, there is a similar genre of stories known as *Immrama*, 'voyage tales'. A number of these tales have saints or clerics as their principal subjects, such as the fabulous 'Wanderings of Colum Cille's Clerics'. The movement of early Irish monks overseas may have led to a synthesis between the traditions of *Immrama* and the traditions of the saints' Lives. To this was also added the ingredient of the Christian 'vision' literature with its fictional descriptions of heaven and hell. The *Navigatio Brendani* has been described as 'the chief single contribution of Ireland to the general literature of medieval Europe'. The *Navigatio* was probably written in the ninth century by an Irishman. During the middle ages, it was translated into Breton, Dutch, Middle English, Flemish, Norman-French, Old French, German, Irish, Italian, Norse, Provencal and Welsh.

The *Navigatio* has been described as 'an amalgam of truth, legend, and literary borrowings'. Several of the stories included in it are paralleled in other mythologies, for example the story of the whale, told below, is similar to that found in the Arabian tale of Sinbad the Sailor.

The *Navigatio* begins with one of Brendan's kinsmen, Barinthus, coming to visit him in Clonfert and giving him an account of his voyage to the 'Island of Delights' and the 'Land of Promise of the Saints'. Brendan decides that he too would have to visit the 'Land of Promise'. After forty days of preparation, he and fourteen companions set out to visit St Enda on Inishmore. From there Brendan journeys to his own home territory in Kerry and 'pitched his tent on the top of a mountain', Mt Brandon (from the top of which, on a clear day, Inishmore is visible). The monks construct their currach in the traditional manner – a timber frame, over which is stretched oak bark covered with tanned ox-hide and greased with animal fat. Along with provisions of food and drink, the monks also store spare skins and fat in case of mishap to the boat.

As the party is about to cast off, three more monks arrive and join them. They set sail 'towards the summer solstice', i.e. to the west. After forty days at sea, 'tormented with hunger and thirst', they spy an island, but have to circle it for three more days before they can land. A dog leads them to a vast hall, where they are served food but are also beset by the 'machinations of the evil one' in the form of a 'little Ethiopian boy'. Later, they are provisioned again by a mysterious young man and once more set sail.

They then encounter a series of islands, including one on which they celebrate the Easter Vigil. However, when they light a fire, the island begins to heave and the monks have to rush back to their boat. The island moves away across the sea and Brendan reveals that it is 'that animal which is greatest of all creatures that swim in the sea'. The whale is called Jasconius, a Latin name almost certainly derived from the Irish word for fish: *iasc*.

The monks then visit an island where there is a tree filled with 'pure white birds'. These turn out to be fallen angels. It is then revealed to Brendan that he and his monks will spend seven years visiting a number of islands in a repeat cycle. They will always spend the Easter Vigil on Jasconius, and spend Christmas on the 'Island of the Community of St Ailbe'.

They travel on, having various other adventures and encounters. One day at sea they encounter a column the colour of silver, harder than marble and made of pure crystal. It is so tall that they can hardly see the top of it. Commentators have suggested that this story represents a real encounter with an iceberg. Later they see a mountain island, vomiting flames and belching smoke, with cliffs that are 'black as coal'. This island (a volcano?), which is a vision of hell, is inhabited by devils. On another island they meet Judas Iscariot, temporarily released from Hell for a 'respite' by his 'loving Saviour'. He gets out of Hell 'from first to second vespers every Sunday, from Christmas to Epiphany, from Easter to Whitsun, and on the feasts of the Purification and the Assumption of the Mother of God.'

Leaving Judas behind them, they travel on. Finally, after seven years, in what is actually something of anti-climax, they arrive at the 'Island of Promise'. Here they gather 'fruit and all kinds of gems', before setting out to return to Ireland. They are told that God delayed their arrival at the island because he first wanted to show them 'the richness of His wonders in the deep'.

The monks now return to Ireland. Brendan's community welcomes him home with great joy; but he has only a short time further to live. Having put his affairs in order, 'he gave up his illustrious spirit to the Lord'.

For a very long time, St Brendan's Isle was thought to have a real geographical existence, sometimes being confused with the Canary Islands or Madeira. Between the sixteenth and eighteenth centuries, various expeditions went in search of it. Famously, the adventurer Tim Severin 'recreated' the saint's voyage and the contemporary composer Shaun Davey, in a further tribute, wrote a musical version of 'The Brendan Voyage'.

The *Annals of Tigernach* records St Brendan's death in the year 575. A poem claims that he was ninety-three years of age when he died. His feast day is marked on 16 May.

> This sage, and prophet, and poet;
> Brendan the saint without crime;
> Ninety-three years exactly,
> Was the length of his perilous time.

11. Saint Kevin

One of the best-known early Irish saints is **St Kevin** of Glendalough. His reputation in modern times is probably based on the fame of the impressive monastic ruins at Glendalough itself, or maybe derives from the humorous ballad about him sung in the late 1960s and 1970s by the group the Dubliners, which suggested a certain misogyny:

> In Glendalough lived an ould saint,
> Who was known for his learning and charity.
> His manners were curious and quaint,
> And he looked upon girls with disparity.

Glendalough – *Gleann dá Locha*, the 'Valley of the Two Lakes' – is an extraordinarily beautiful place in the centre of the Wicklow mountains. It has long been a place of contemplation and pilgrimage. In fact, remains of a medieval 'pilgrim road' leading over the mountains to the valley from the significantly named Holywood (*Cillín Chaoimhín* in Irish, 'Kevin's little church'), have been discovered and excavated. However, the numerous early monastic and ecclesiastical buildings in the valley itself date to a much later period than the time of St Kevin. The only feature in the valley which might be said with confidence to date from the age of the saint, the cave known as 'Kevin's Bed', might actually belong to an even earlier period, perhaps the Bronze Age, thousands of years before Jesus, never mind St Kevin.

As its name indicates, the valley contains two lakes. The larger is known as the Upper Lake, the smaller known as the Lower Lake. Kevin almost certainly founded his place of retreat on the shores of the Upper Lake, near where the present ruins known as Temple na Skellig and Reefert

Church now stand. The remains of a number of other structures of an apparently early date have been found in this area also. It appears that over the centuries as the monastery grew in strength, a decision was taken to move the settlement down the valley, to a more level area east of the Lower Lake, where a relatively large monastic 'city' was developed. This is where we can now find most of the major monuments: the formal and unique gateway into the complex, the round tower, the cathedral, St Kevin's Kitchen (in fact a church), as well as a number of other monuments and structures of the early medieval period.

In the Lives, Kevin's birth is foretold with a typical hagiographical flourish:

> There would come a high saint, honourable and noble ... to rescue and repel men from paganism by the preaching of the word of God, for the healing of lepers, and blind, and deaf, and lame, and all kinds of sick people, to raise the dead, to put down the mighty and lift up the wretched, and to drive away plagues and pestilences, to check thieves and crimes and strange monsters, and to instruct all kinds of perverted persons who opposed the will of God.

The name Kevin (in old Irish Cáemgen or Cóemgen) means something like 'beautiful birth' or 'comely baby'. He was probably born in the middle of the sixth century. The hagiographers claimed that his mother did not suffer the 'pains of labour or pangs of childbearing'. He belonged to an aristocratic Leinster family. His genealogy as outlined in the Lives suggests that he was related to **St Colum mac Crimthann**, the founder of the monastery of Terryglass, County Tipperary, whose feast day is 13 December. However, it has also been suggested that this Colum and his more famous namesake, the founder of Iona, were in actuality the same person. At any rate, Kevin was baptised by 'the noble honourable patron saint,

Cronan'. There are about twenty saints of that name but it is not clear which if any of them is referred to here.

Kevin is supposed to have received his early education and to have been ordained at the monastery of Kilnamanagh in Wicklow, founded by **St Eoghan of Ardstraw** (now in County Tyrone). St Eoghan (anglicised as Eugene from the Latin form Eugenius) is the patron of the Diocese of Derry. He is reputed to have been captured by pirates and taken to Britain. He eventually escaped and went to study at the monastery of Whithorn in Galloway. From there he came to Ireland, first founding Kilnamanagh and later going north. St Eoghan's feast day is 23 August.

In the Latin Life of Kevin, it is claimed that he first founded the church at *Cluain Duach*, possibly near Holywood, County Wicklow. Kevin then went as a hermit to the lonely valley of Glendalough, living, we are told, in Kevin's Bed, a cliff cave high above the Upper Lake. As was to be expected, Kevin attracted many followers and soon a larger settlement had to be set up.

Many of the stories about Kevin reflect a special relationship with nature. These have been compared to the stories about St Francis of Assisi. Kevin is also said to have dressed in the skins of wild animals. One story tells of how, when performing the ascetic practice of praying while standing up to his waste in the water of the lough, Kevin one day dropped his psalter into the lake and an otter retrieved it for him. We are told that snow avoided Kevin's pastures, so that his animals could continue to graze there in winter. When Kevin was being carried honourably through the woods on a litter, the trees would lie down so as to make a pathway for him; 'rising up again in their natural fashion' when the saint had passed. Kevin is credited with having the power to make plants grow out of season. One story tells of how once when he was engaged in the Irish practice of 'cross-vigil' (i.e. praying with the arms outstretched, in the form of a cross), a blackbird came and built a nest in his hand and laid her eggs there. Kevin remained with his arm outstretched until the bird had hatched her brood. Another story tells how Kevin banished a monster out of the upper, into the lower, lake. This monster had been wreaking havoc since the time of the Fianna. The vacated lake then became a 'sacred wonder-working lough', a source of many cures:

> ... the place where now help of every trouble is wrought both for men and cattle; and they all leave their sicknesses [in the lake] and these sicknesses and diseases go into the other lake to [weaken] the monster so that it does not injure anyone.

The Lives are quite mercenary in promoting Glendalough as a place of pilgrimage, healings and miracles; presumably these wonders resulted in suitable donations being made to the church. To make seven pilgrimages to Glendalough is claimed to be equivalent to making one pilgrimage to Rome. Kevin can rescue nine souls every Saturday from the pains of Hell, and everyone 'who shall die on Friday and be buried on a Saturday under the mould of Kevin [i.e. in the clay of Glendalough] shall receive remission for his soul.' No wonder the authorities find it difficult, even today, to restrict burial inside the graveyard at the heart of the main monastic site in Glendalough. Before he died, Kevin left a protection to his monastery from plunder and ravaging:

> He promised punishment for all these things, to wit, short life, and hell at the last. And he chose these four diseases to wreak vengeance on the body of every one who should outrage his church, or his successors, or his congregation; namely tumour, scrofula, anthrax, and madness; and no leech or physician can cure these diseases, save only the Healer, Jesus Christ.

Kevin's death is entered in the *Annals of Tigernach* at 617. His feast day is 3 June. This date was marked as a great occasion at Glendalough from early times right down to the nineteenth century, long after the valley had ceased to be a centre of population. The *patrún* ('patron') day was suppressed in 1862 by the Ultramontane Catholic Cardinal Cullen, but not before something of its excitement had been captured in 1817 by the artist Joseph Peacock in his painting 'The Festival of St Kevin at the Seven Churches, Glendalough'.

A near contemporary of Kevin was **St Colmán Ela**. St Colmán is said to have belonged to the Dál nAraide of what is now County Antrim, and is associated in stories with **St Mac Nisse** (feast day 3 September), patron of the Diocese of Connor. Colmán is reckoned in some sources to be the second patron of Connor. Colmán was born in the 550s, as he was said to be fifty-six when he died in 609. He was founder of the church of *Lann-Elo*, the 'House of Elo', from which he took the second part of his name. *Lann-Elo* is now Lynally, County Offaly.

Adomnán tells us that Colmán visited Colum Cille at Iona a year before the latter's death. Kilcalmonell in Argyle and Colmonell in Ayrshire are named after him. To Colmán is attributed the spiritual tract known as *Apgitir Chrábaid*, the 'Alphabet of Piety'. One beautiful story, which is also told about other saints, is related of Colmán: He had three 'brother monks' – a cock, a mouse and a fly. The cock, of course, would waken him from sleep in the morning, the mouse would make sure he didn't fall asleep again by nibbling his ear, and the fly would mark his place in a book if Colmán had to leave off reading it. A story in his Irish Life reveals how some Irish monastic graveyards were designated as 'Rome burials', i.e. burial there was believed to be the same for indulgence purposes as being buried in Rome, helping to speed the deceased on their way to Heaven.

Colmán was sent a present from the pope of 'seven asses laden with seven sacks full of the soil of Rome'. The soil was spread over the cemetery, in effect 'Romanising' it. Anyone who was buried in the cemetery after that would 'not see hell'. The monks from the nearby monastery of Durrow were jealous and came to steal some of the precious clay. Colmán was furious, but when Colum Cille, who had founded the monastery at Durrow, arrived from Iona and apologised, Colmán said that they could keep the clay, and 'I pray to God that it may have for you the virtue of the earth of Rome from henceforth.'

Colmán's feast day is 26 September. In one old verse, he is credited with being the patron saint of horseback riding.

12. St Máedóc or St Aidan

In the early Christian period, Ferns was the chief church of the people called Uí Cennselaig (Kinsella), who ruled, more or less, what is now County Wexford. Ferns had displaced the previously significant monastery of Mag Arnaide, founded by the very early St Abbán, as the chief church of southern Leinster. The founder of Ferns was said to be a bishop called Áed, a name which has come down to us in a variety of hypocoristic forms – Áedán, Mo-Áed-óc, Máedóc or, in modern Irish, Maodhóg. These names have been anglicised as Aidan and Maodhog (pronounced Mwee-ogue), or locally in Wexford and elsewhere as Mogue (the second of these forms giving us the place name *Buaile Mhaodhóg*, the 'Boolavogue' of the well-known song of that name which commemorates the 1798 Rebellion). Several other churches in Leinster claimed to have been founded by **St Máedóc** as well. There were also churches in the Cavan/Leitrim area, the ancient territory of Breifne, which were associated with Máedóc. Of these, the most important were Drumlane and Rossinver.

There are several Lives of Máedóc, both in Latin and Irish, but they give us very little useful information about the actual life of the saint. His alleged birthplace was on 'St Mogue's Island' in Templeport Lough, County Cavan. There are several traditions about his genealogical background, including one that asserts that he belonged to the Uí Meic Cáirthinn, a small and relatively unimportant group of people who lived along the east bank of the River Foyle, opposite Derry. Another tradition is that he was the son of a king of Connacht, whose sanctity was predicted even before his birth.

As a young man he was praying once, with his close friend Lasrianus, beneath two trees. One of the trees fell towards the south, the other towards the north. 'The fall of the trees reveals that we must part,' they said, and so Máedóc went south to Ferns, while Lasrianus went north to found the monastery on Devenish Island in Lough Erne, County Fermanagh. Lasrianus is better known by the Irish hypocoristic form of his name, **St Molaisse**. His feast day is 12 September. His death is entered in the *Annals of Tigernach* at 562. He seems, therefore, to have been too early to have been a contemporary of Máedóc. The story of the trees probably reflects some later agreement between the two monasteries mentioned.

The similarly-named **St Molaisse** of Inishmurray (feast day 12 August) may actually be the same person. Inishmurray is an island about four miles off the coast of County Sligo, where remarkable remains of an ancient monastery still survive. The island takes its name from its founding saint **Muiredach** (feast day also 12 August or 13 August). Inishmurray is one of the best preserved ancient monasteries from the early Christian period in Ireland. The site is enclosed by a massive dry stone wall, up to four metres in height, which is pierced by a number of entrances. There are also a number of chambers inside this wall, and flights of steps lead to the top parapet. Internally the pear-shaped space, which measures about fifty-eight metres by forty-four metres, is divided into three sections. Inside, there are a number of 'altars', church buildings and clocháns, or stone huts. On one of the altars can be found the *Clocha Breaca*, or 'Speckled Stones', which in the past were used for 'cursing' enemies.

Outside the enclosure there are several other ecclesiastical buildings and monuments, including a fine collection of cross-slabs. All of these were incorporated in the traditional pilgrimage route around the island. This so-called 'Big Station' took place annually on the Feast of the Assumption, 15 August; for those not able to make the full circuit, there was also a 'Wee Station'. A striking thirteenth-century wooden statue, said to depict St Molaisse and now in the National Museum of Ireland, used to be housed in Teach Molaisse (Molaisse's House), inside the enclosure.

According to the Lives, after parting with Lasrianus, Máedóc went to study with St David in Wales and, on his return, the king of Uí Cennselaig gave him Ferns as the site for a church. Once, Máedóc was building a church but he couldn't find a mason. So he blessed the hands of one of his followers named Gobán. Gobán built the church 'with wondrous carvings, and brave ornaments, that there was not the like of it anywhere, and no one in his time surpassed this Gobán in his craft.' This Gobán is, of course, the thinly disguised Gobán Saor, the famous craftsman of Irish legend and folklore, who appears in many stories and is associated with a number of other Leinster saints.

One of the Lives of Máedóc, in Irish, is a very large and detailed work, containing around 50,000 words of prose and verse (that's nearly twice as large as this book). In the Life, Máedóc's miracles don't even wait for his birth. Both his mother and father see visions which foretell the coming of the holy child. Other miracles follow on immediately after he is born. He was fostered by an O'Duffey family, and it was they who are said to have habitually called him 'my little Áed' or *M'Áed óc*.

Máedóc was taken as a hostage by the 'King of Ireland', Ainmire mac Sétna, in order to ensure his father's loyalty, but the king, recognising the sanctity of the boy, released him. Máedóc's piety continued to grow and he planned to make a pilgrimage to Rome 'to acquire carefully knowledge and expertness in the divine Scripture, as other saints and devotees were wont to do at that time.' He took with him three other saints: the Molaisse mentioned above, **St Caillin of Fenagh**, County Leitrim (feast day 13 November; said to be a contemporary of Colum Cille and 'faithful foster-father' of Máedóc), and **St Ultan of Ardbraccan**, near Navan in County Meath (feast day 4 September; he actually died in 656, almost 100 years after the death of Maedóc). Ultan is said to be the composer of a beautiful hymn about St Brigid:

> Brigid excellent woman,
> Golden sparkling flame,
> Lead us to eternal heaven,
> The dazzling sun, our aim.

This story shows the complete indifference to the facts of chronology on the part of the hagiographer, just as we find in many of the other Lives of the saints. At any rate, the four saints are said to have spent a year together in Rome and three of them, including Máedóc, were ordained as bishops. On his return to Ireland, Aed, the king of Uí Briúin in Connacht, came to Máedóc and asked the bishop to change his (the king's) appearance because 'up to that time he was hideous' to look at. Aed was put asleep with his face under Máedóc's cloak and 'the form which he put upon him was [that of] the one most beautiful man of all the men of Ireland in his time'.

As a result of this miracle, the kings of Uí Briúin owed a great deal of tribute to Máedóc and his successors at Drumlane and Rossinver, including 'the horse and robes of the king of Breifne on his coronation day ... or else ten horses or twenty cattle'. If there is any failure to deliver this tribute, the family (i.e. the monks) of Máedóc must curse the king in a process involving ritual fasting (hunger striking) and the turning 'widdershins' or anticlockwise of the *Breac Máedóc* (the elaborate relic shrine of Máedóc, now in the National Museum). 'Short life and hell is the inevitable lot of every one who earns the curse'. Máedóc later set up his church at Drumlane, where the *Breac Máedóc* was traditionally kept.

Máedóc then went study with St David in Wales, where he performed more miracles. Among the stories told about his stay in Wales is one in which Máedóc is asked to bless the army of the Britons, who are about to confront the invading Saxons. The Britons, of course, had the victory, 'through the favour of God and the miracles of Máedóc.'

He then returned to Ireland and founded the church of *Ard Ladrann* (possibly Ardamine near Courtown, County Wexford). He also founded churches at *Dísert nDairbre*, near Ardmore in County Waterford, and *Cluain Dicholla*, near Enniscorthy in County Wexford, as well as performing miracles all over south Leinster. Later, the king of Leinster, Brandubh son of Eochaid (died 603), in payment for another one of Máedóc's miracles, granted the monk the site of *Ferna Mór Máedóc* – Ferns, County Wexford. There was also a monastery called *Cluain Mór Máedóc* near Rathvilly in County Carlow.

Like some of the other early saints, Máedóc is said to have worn 'clothes made of the skins of brute beasts and wild animals'. One day as they walked along a road, Máedóc's servant asked him who would succeed him when he died. 'Whoever opens that gate ahead of us,' he said. 'They saw coming towards them a troop of wanton restless scholars [schoolboys] with toy shields and spears, playing and hurling together.' One of the scholars, Moling Luachra, opened the gate.

St Moling was claimed as another patron of Leinster. He became a bishop at Ferns and also, allegedly of

Glendalough. He founded his own church at *Tech Moling,* 'Moling's House' – St Mullins, on a promontory above the River Barrow, County Carlow. St Mullins remained a place of pilgrimage for a long time but, as usual, little remains from the early monastery except the stump of a round tower and a granite high cross. The Book of Mulling (or Moling) is an eighth- or ninth-century manuscript, essentially a copy of the four Gospels. Uniquely, it contains a drawing of what appears to be the plan of an early Irish monastery. Moling is credited with ending the *bórama* ('cattle tribute'), which the kings of Leinster were obliged to pay to the kings of Tara. A collection of poems and other texts are attributed to Moling, but they actually belong to the eleventh century and later. Moling died in 697. His feast day is 17 June.

The long Life of Máedóc grandiosely describes him as *Erlamh Eorpa,* 'Patron saint of Europe'. Near the time of his death, the saint is said to have gone to Rossinver in County Fermanagh, his place of 'resurrection'. He asks Dallán Forgail – 'a poet, a prophet, and a true saint' – to come and witness his will. Dallán is said in some sources to have been Máedóc's cousin. He was a famous poet, the author of the *Amra Coluim Chille,* 'Eulogy of Colum Cille', and, as mentioned above, was also venerated as a saint. A **St Dallán** with a feast day on 14 December is recorded, but it is not certain that this is the same person. At any rate, when the time came for Dallán to leave Máedóc, he was:

> ... sorrowful, sad, and melancholy ... it was, moreover, like the separation of a woman from her son, or a cow from her calf, or a bitch from her pups, or a duck from her pool, the parting of them one from the other at that time.'

The Life finishes with a baroque description of Máedóc's death:

> The last day of his age and time drew near, as his guardian and assisting angel had revealed to him. There came ten and three times fifty saints and holy virgins to the scene of his death and departure, and he received the Communion and sacrifice from them ... and he sent his spirit to heaven among the saints and holy angels, after conquering the world and the devil, on the last day of January precisely.

> There came then wondrous great hosts of angels to meet him, and to convey his soul with melodious songs, and marvellous sweet organs, and musical and moving cries.

The Life continues by describing the miracles that occurred after the saint's death. The *Annals of Tigernach* records Máedóc's death in both of the years 626 and 659, so it is possible that traditions of two separate individuals have been conflated in the stories about him. His feast day is 31 January.

Another well-known saint with a variation of the name Áed was **St Áed mac Bricc**. This Áed belonged to the southern Uí Néill, that is the people of the Meath/Westmeath area. His church was at Killare in Westmeath, but he was also associated with Sliabh League, the extraordinary mountain sea cliffs in southwest Donegal, on the top of which he is supposed to have had a hermitage. Áed is referred to in the annals as a bishop, but he was also known as a *sui-liag*, a 'master physician'. It was believed that his intercession could obtain the curing of headaches. His death is entered in the *Annals of Tigernach* at the year 587. His feast day is 10 November.

13. St Columbanus and his Disciples

Christianity had spread throughout western Europe to a great extent during the fourth and fifth centuries, as it had become the official religion of the expansionist Roman Empire. As that empire collapsed and withdrew, from the second part of the fifth century onwards, partly as a result of the invasions of the so-called Germanic tribes – the Franks, the Ostrogoths, the Visigoths, the Huns, and so on – former Christian areas largely reverted to paganism.

Paradoxically, in Ireland, which had not been part of the Empire and where Christianity had come comparatively late, the new religion survived and flourished. So it was that missionaries from this country came to play a significant role in the re-Christianisation of Europe from the late sixth century onwards. This role has often been exaggerated in the past, but Irish missionaries were extraordinarily influential in the return of Christianity to this part of the continent. Many of the clerics who took part in these missions were later remembered as saints.

St Columbanus, also known as Columban (another variation on the name Colum/Columba), was one of the greatest and most influential of the Irish monks who went to the continent of Europe.

Columbanus was born in Leinster about 543. Around 560 he is said to have gone as a novice to the monastery of Cleenish on Lough Erne, allegedly founded shortly before by **St Sinell** (feast day 11 November). Sinell is said to have studied with St Finnian of Clonard and in some versions is included among the 'twelve apostles of Ireland'. At length, Columbanus decided to become a monk and went further north, to the monastery at Bangor founded by **St Comgall**. Bangor, on the southern shore of Belfast Lough, now in

County Down, was established about 557. Comgall belonged to the local people, the Dál nAraide, and was born around 515. His death is recorded in 600 and his feast day is 10 May. The monastery at Bangor became one of the most important ecclesiastical centres in the country. It was noted for its strict rule and ascetic practices and these seem to have had a particular influence on Columbanus. The *Antiphonary of Bangor,* the late seventh-century manuscript now in the Ambrosian Library in Milan, is one of the most significant manuscripts from the early Irish church.

After some years in Bangor, Columbanus approached Comgall, seeking his permission to go abroad. Comgall at first refused, but later relented and Columbanus, together with twelve followers, set out. This figure of twelve companions appears in the stories of several Irish saints: for example, Colum Cille is said to have taken twelve companions with him to Iona. Historians have debated whether this is a fictional, formulaic figure or whether it represents the individuals in question consciously following the model of Jesus and the twelve apostles. It is difficult to come to a conclusion on the matter.

Because of some contradictions in historical sources, there are differences of opinion as to when Columbanus went to Gaul. 591 is an accepted date, but some have argued for a date as early as the 570s. Again, depending on which interpretation is taken, the king of the territories of Austrasia and Burgundy, to which Columbanus went, was either Sigebert (died 575) or Gunthram (died 593). Whichever king it was, he welcomed the strangers and begged them to stay in his kingdom. The monks explored the mountainous and thickly-forested Vosges area, and finally settled on the ruins of an old Roman fort, at Annegray in the valley of the River Breuchen, as a site for their monastery. They repaired the abandoned Temple of Diana in the fort and refurbished it as a church, significantly dedicating it to St Martin of Tours – a European saint, as mentioned before, who was greatly revered in the Irish church.

Crowds flocked to the monastery, but Columbanus found a cave nearby which served him as a hermitage for private meditation and prayer. The number of monks began to increase and so a second monastery was founded, eight miles away at another old Roman fort, in a place called Luxeuil. Later, a third house was founded, three miles away from Luxeuil, at Fontaine. Eventually Luxeuil became the principal foundation of the three. These monasteries adhered to the Irish customs that the monks had brought with them. Some of these customs, such as the calculation of the date of Easter, differed from the rest of the church. Columbanus wrote to Pope Gregory the Great about the Easter issue. He speaks to the pope in phrases which gives us some insight into his confident manner, as well as his sense of humour:

> When an unworthy man like me writes to an illustrious one like yourself, my insignificance makes applicable to me the striking remark which a certain philosopher is said to have once made on seeing a painted harlot: 'I do not admire the art, but I admire the cheek'...
>
> Everyone knows my demands are pressing, my enquiries wide. But your resources are also great, for you know well that from a small stock less should be lent, and 'from a large one more'.
>
> (trans: Tomás Ó Fiaich)

Columbanus fell foul of the royal family when he criticised the lifestyle of Thierry, the new king of Burgundy. As a consequence, he and his Irish monks were expelled from Luxeuil and ordered to leave Gaul. On their very eventful journey to the coast to take a ship, one of the monks – Deicolus or

Dicuil, who had come from Ireland with Columbanus but was now very old and feeble – left the party, unable to continue. He founded a monastery at Lure in the valley of the Oignon, Haute Saone. Several hundred years after his death, a monk from this monastery wrote his Life. He was venerated as a saint, with a feast day on 16 January.

After leaving Deicolus, Columbanus's party continued on, sailing down the Loire and stopping to spend a night at the tomb of St Martin, in Tours. Finally they reached the port at Nantes, but the ship they were to sail on could not leave because of a storm. Taking this as a sign from God that they were not to leave Gaul, the captain put the party ashore again. Columbanus now set out on another epic journey, travelling on the rivers Moselle and the Rhine and its tributaries, down into what is now Switzerland. Perhaps from this period is derived one of the poems attributed to Columbanus, the '*Carmen Navale*' or 'Boat Song', from which the beginning and final sections are quoted below:

> En silvis caesa fluctu meat acta carina
> Bicornis Hreni et pelagus perlabitur uncta.
> Heia viri! nostrum reboans echo sonet heia!
>
> Lo, little bark on twin horned Rhine
> From forests hew to skim the brine,
> Heave, lads, and let the echoes ring ...
>
> Rex quoque virtutum, rerum fons, summa potestas,
> Certanti spondet, vincenti praemia donat.
> Vestra, viri, Christum memorans mens personet heia!
>
> The King of virtue vowed a prize
> For him who wins, for him who tries,
> Think, lads, of Christ and echo him.
>
> *(trans: Tomás Ó Fiaich)*

The party eventually arrived at Bregenz on Lake Constance, where they stopped for about a year. Finally, in 612, Columbanus decided to move on, but one of the Irish who had come with him originally from Bangor wished to remain. This was **St Gall**, who had been very active converting the local people and raising controversy by destroying their wooden idols. Gall established a hermitage and was joined by some other monks. He died about 630 and, about 720, the great Benedictine abbey of Sankt Gallen was established on the site of his refuge. This abbey was not an Irish monastery in any sense, but it is clear that many Irishmen settled there or visited it, perhaps while going or returning from a pilgrimage to Rome. Sankt Gallen's famous library, built up for the most part in the ninth century, contained a significant collection of *Scottice scripti*, or Irish books.

St Gall was venerated as one of the patron saints of Switzerland and his feast day is celebrated on 16 October.

Having left Gall behind him, and despite the fact that he was about seventy years of age by this time, Columbanus made his way over the Alps into Italy and the court of the kings of Lombardy at Milan. From Milan, in 613 Columbanus wrote a famous letter to Pope Boniface IV. The letter deals mainly with the subject of the heresy which the pope had been accused of, but also strongly proclaims the orthodoxy of the Irish church:

> For all we Irish, inhabitants of the world's edge, are disciples of Saints Peter and Paul and of all the disciples who wrote the sacred canon by the Holy Spirit. We accept nothing outside the evangelical and apostolic teaching. None of us was a heretic, no one a Jew [i.e. in the matter of the calculation of the date of Easter], no one a schismatic; but the Catholic Faith, as it was first transmitted by you (the Popes), successors of the holy apostles, is maintained unbroken.

> *(trans: Tomás Ó Fiaich)*

The king of Lombardy offered Columbanus a ruined church dedicated to St Peter about seventy miles south of Milan. In 614 the monastery of Bobbio was founded there, another Irish continental institution which was to become very famous. Paradoxically, shortly before his death, messengers came to Bobbio inviting the elderly monk to return as abbot to Luxeuil; the local political situation there having altered considerably in the meantime. Columbanus declined, and died at Bobbio in 615. His feast day is 23 November.

Three years after the death of Columbanus, Jonas, a young monk from the Piedmont district of northern Italy, entered the monastery at Bobbio (paradoxically the name 'Jonas' is a form of the Hebrew word which, like the Latin name Columbanus, meant 'dove'). Jonas became secretary to Columbanus's successor as abbot, Attala. Later he spent many years travelling around the continent, collecting stories and details of Columbanus's life as he went. Sometime around 640, at the request of his brother monks in Bobbio and their abbot, he wrote 'an account of the life and work of our beloved father Columbanus, particularly as so many of those who had lived with him and seen his work were still alive.'

Jonas's Life of Columbanus is our chief source of information for the life of this saint, who Robert Schuman, the architect of post-war European unity, once described as 'the patron saint of those who seek to construct a united Europe.'

As Tomás Ó Fiaich said, 'before his death much of western Europe was dotted with monasteries founded by Columban[us]'s disciples.' The principal editor and translator of Columbanus's writings, GSM Walker, summed up this complicated individual in his book *Sancti Columbani Opera* as follows:

A character so complex and so contrary, humble and haughty, harsh and tender, pedantic and impetuous by turns, had as its guiding and unifying pattern the ambition of sainthood. All his activities were subordinate to this one end, and with the self-sacrifice that can seem so close to self-assertion, he worked out his soul's salvation by the one sure pathway that he knew. He was a missionary through circumstance, a monk by vocation; a contemplative, too frequently driven to action by the world; a pilgrim, on the road to Paradise.

14. Other Irish Saints on the Continent

The historian Richard Sharpe, who has worked extensively on the Lives of Irish saints, has remarked, that 'so great was the impact of the Irish on European ideas of sainthood that it became a common motif in hagiography to ascribe to almost any little known saint an Irish birthright.' However, only a few of the very many continental saints of alleged Irish origin can be discussed here.

One of the best-known Irish saints in continental Europe was **St Fursa**, or Fursey as his name is often anglicised. Fursa belonged to the first half of the seventh century, the generation after that of Columbanus. We know quite a lot about Fursa from the writings of the Venerable Bede and from a number of Lives of him which survive. St Fursa's Visions of Heaven and Hell, one of the earliest examples of this genre of literature, became very popular all over Europe. It influenced much of the kind of medieval religious thought which, as has been frequently pointed out, later found its ultimate expression in Dante's *The Divine Comedy*.

Bede tells us that Fursa was of noble Irish origin and, having studied the sacred books, founded a monastery in Ireland. At this monastery he became ill. Falling into a trance, his spirit left his body from sunset to cockcrow, during which time he saw many visions. Three days later he had a similar experience. This second time, as well as seeing choirs of angels and the hosts of the blessed in Heaven, he was attacked by evil spirits who struggled to keep him away from Heaven. When the angels had taken him up to a great height, he looked back at the world and saw four fires in the air. The angels told him that these were the fires which would consume the earth: Falsehood, Covetousness,

Discord and Cruelty. In the vision, the four fires merged into a huge conflagration. Fursa's vision also included many other examples of the works of the devil. Bede tells us that he had heard the account of Fursa's visions from an old monk in his own monastery, who, in turn, had heard it from a 'truthful and devout' man who had heard them in East Anglia, related by Fursa himself.

From his monastery, Fursa preached the word of God among the Irish for many years, but he found it hard to endure the crowds of the faithful that thronged about him. He resolved to abandon everything and, taking a few companions with him, he crossed over to England about the year 630. King Sigbert of the East Angles made him welcome and Fursa began preaching there. Bede tells us that Fursa's goodness was so inspiring that many were converted to Christianity by him and many who already believed had their faith strengthened. King Sigbert gave him, as the site for a monastery, an old ruined fortification at a pleasant location in woods close to the sea. This was Cnobheresburg or Burgh Castle, near Yarmouth. The local aristocracy also endowed the monastery with fine buildings and other gifts.

Again Fursa is said to have grown restless, longing to be rid of worldly business, even the business of the monastery. He entrusted the monastery to his brother **Foillan** (feast day 30 October) and set out to become a hermit. Fursa had another brother, **Ultán** (feast days: 2 May – the day of his death in 686 – and 31 October), who was a hermit. Fursa sought Ultán out and began to share his life of prayer and austerity. This period of his life lasted for one year. At the end of that year he sailed over to Gaul (France), where he was welcomed by King Clovis II and the Neustrian 'mayor of the palace', Erchinoald. The Frankish territory of Neustria consisted of the central and western part of Gaul.

Erchinoald granted Fursa a site for a monastery at Lagny, on the River Marne near Paris. Fursa died in 649/650 and Erchinoald had his body (which, apparently, had remained uncorrupted) placed in a tomb about 654, at a new church he had built at Péronne in Picardy, in northern France. Fursa's feast day was 16 January. It is worth pointing out that the highly entertaining, satirical comic novels by the Irish writer Mervyn Wall, *The Unfortunate Fursey* (1946), *The Return of Fursey* (1948) and *The Complete Fursey* (1985), do not deal with the saint of this name, but with a 'simple--minded' monk from Clonmacnoise whose cell is invaded by the devil.

The tomb of Saint Fursa became a major pilgrimage destination, and was known as *Perrona Scottorum* ('Péronne of the Irish'). Thus was inaugurated, as one historian has put it, 'the heyday of Irish influence in Picardy and Flanders'. Foillan and Ultán, Fursa's two brothers, later became abbots at Péronne, as did other Irishmen. Péronne continued as an Irish institution until at least the end of the eighth century, and maybe as late as 880 when it was destroyed by Vikings. Foillan subsequently left Péronne and went to Nivelles (in modern Belgium). Ita the abbess of Nivelles, which was apparently run along Irish lines, gave land at nearby Fosses to Foillan to establish a monastery. He was murdered by robbers about the year 655. One tradition claims that he was succeeded as abbot of Fosses by his brother Ultán.

St Fiacre is another Irish hermit of the mid-seventh century whose cult was widespread in France. Having come from Ireland (we do not know the date), he set up a hermitage at Meaux, east of Paris, and a hospice for travellers at what is now the town of Saint-Fiacre-en-Brie. He is said to have been rigorous in excluding women from his hermitage, which ultimately grew into the monastery of Breuil. Because of the reputed excellence of the vegetables he

grew, Fiacre is known in France as a patron saint of garden-
ers. His cult also had many associations with the cure of
sickness, and his intercession was invoked particularly by
those suffering from syphilis and from haemorrhoids;
indeed, the latter disorder was known as the '*mal de Saint
Fiacre*'. The name *Fiacre* also became attached to a type of
four-wheeled carriage, available for public hire in Paris from
around 1620. The terminus for these carriages was close to
the Hotel Saint-Fiacre, hence the association with the saint's
name. St Fiacre died about 670 and his feast day is celebrated on 30 August or 1 September.

The land at Breuil had been given to Fiacre by St Faro,
or Burgundofaro, the bishop of Meaux who died around
672. His brother, St Cagnoald, is said to have been one of
Columbanus's monks at Luxeuil. A Life of St Faro was
written in the mid-ninth century by one of his successors,
Hildegaire. Hildegaire also wrote a life of another mid-
seventh-century saint, the Irish hermit **Kilian of
Aubigny**. St Faro is said to have persuaded Kilian to settle
at Aubigny, near Arras.

There is another Irish **St Kilian**; of Wurzburg in Germany. This Irish bishop went to the continent with eleven
companions, and worked in Thuringia and the eastern parts
of the Frankish kingdoms. Kilian was murdered about 689,
and the first bishop of Wurzburg, Burchard, had his relics
'translated' to the cathedral there in 752.

Around 742 an Irishman named **Virgil** (probably originally some form of the name Fergal) went to Gaul and
onwards to Bavaria. Although it is sometimes suggested that
the person in question was the abbot of the monastery of
Aghaboe in County Laois, whose death is recorded in 784 or
789, it is much more likely that we are dealing with a different cleric who had earlier been a monk in one of the Columban monasteries, possibly Iona. Virgil eventually became

abbot of the monastery of St Peter in Salzburg. Somewhat unexpectedly, the 'confraternity book' of that monastery contains a list of the abbots of Iona, almost certainly reflecting some of Virgil's older connections. From his position as abbot, Virgil took over the running of the local diocese and in 755 he was formally consecrated as the bishop of that diocese. He is remembered especially as the evangeliser of the province of Carinthia.

It appears that Virgil was something of a controversialist, and came into conflict with the Englishman St Boniface. On a number of occasions, Virgil was reported to Pope Zachary. In a letter from the Pope dated 1 May 748, it is suggested that Virgil might be excommunicated if the charge be upheld that he is a believer in the doctrine of the antipodes – 'that there are another world and other men under the earth'. However, nothing more is heard about this accusation. Despite this difficulty, Virgil was officially canonised as a saint in 1233, one of only a handful of such saints from this country. His feast day was 27 November, the date of his death, possibly in the year 784.

The small city of Fiesole, near Florence, commemorates another Irish saint – **St Donatus**. Not very much is known about his Irish background, but Donatus was probably born in the early part of the ninth century. He is said to have studied at the monastery on Scattery Island in the Shannon Estuary, but to have left after a Viking raid there and made a pilgrimage to Rome. On his way back he passed through Fiesole, where the local bishop had just died. Donatus was miraculously indicated as the appropriate successor. Around 850, he is said to have given the church and hospice at Piacenza, named after St Brigid, to Columbanus's abbey at Bobbio. He is remembered as a poet and his homesickness is said to be reflected in the following Latin verses:

The noblest share of earth is the far western world
Whose name is written Scottia [Ireland] in the ancient books;
Rich in goods, in silver, jewels, cloth and gold,
Benign to the body, in air and mellow soil ...
There no poison harms, no serpent glides in the grass,
No frog harshly sings his loud complaint in the lake.
Worthy are the Irish to dwell in this their land,
A race of men renowned in war, in peace, in faith.

(trans: Liam de Paor)

Donatus died in 876. His relics are preserved in Fiesole cathedral and his feast day is 22 October.

In 1012 an Irish monk called Colmán was beaten to death at Stockerau, just north of Vienna, while making a pilgrimage to the Holy Land. The emperor Henry II erected a special tomb for Colomann, as he became known, at Melk, on the Danube east of Vienna. A Life of this Irishman was written, and he came to be honoured as one of the patron saints of Austria. As Kálmán, his cult passed into Hungary, where there was also considerable devotion to him.

15. St Malachy and his Associates

St Malachy of Armagh is one of the handful of Irish saints to have been officially canonised. He was one of the great reformers of the church in twelfth-century Ireland and a friend of the even more famous St Bernard of Clarvaux, one of the founders of the Cistercian order of monks. St Bernard later wrote a Life of St Malachy.

Malachy's name in Irish was Mael Máedóc Ua Morgair (despite its Irish appearance, Malachy is a version of the Old Testament name Malachias). The term *mael* meant 'bald' or 'shaved', the original reference being to the practice of monastic tonsuring, the ritual shaving of hair from part of the head as a visible sign of dedication to the service of God. In this context it meant something like 'follower' or 'devotee' of. In early Irish personal names, the element Mael (as also the element *Giolla,* meaning 'Servant of') was often accompanied by the name of a saint such as Mael Pátraic, literally 'follower of Patrick', or Mael Bríde, 'follower of Brigid'. Thus Mael Máedóc meant 'follower of St Máedóc'.

Malachy was born in the year 1094 at Armagh, into a family with a major local reputation for learning. When he died in 1102, Mugrón, Malachy's father, was described as the *ard fer leighind* or 'chief lector of Armagh and of all western Europe'. Malachy's mother's family was apparently connected with the monastery at Bangor in County Down. Malachy was one of three children. His younger brother, **Giolla Críst** (literally, 'Servant of Christ'), also became a cleric and was known as a distinguished preacher. He was appointed bishop of Clogher by Malachy in 1135, but was buried in Armagh when he died in 1138, at about forty years of age. He, also, was venerated as a saint, with a feast day on 12 June.

This was a time when the Irish church was undergoing major reforms, both in terms of church discipline and of organisation. It had been clear for some time that at least in some respects the Irish church was out of step with contemporary practices in the rest of Christendom. Marriage practices in Ireland, for example, included in some cases polygamy, marriage between blood relatives and divorce. The Irish church had originally been heavily influenced by monasticism and in some cases these ancient monasteries, and particularly the senior offices of the monastery, had become secularised. The structure of the church, particularly the role of bishops, was very out of step with practice elsewhere. Out of the reform movement of the late eleventh and early twelfth centuries would come the diocesan system, which by and large has endured down to the present day in both the Church of Ireland and the Roman Catholic Church.

As a young man, Malachy went to join the ascetic Imar Ua hAedacáin, abbot of the monastery of SS Peter and Paul in Armagh. In 1119, at twenty-five years of age (five years younger than was allowed by canon law), he was ordained a priest in Armagh. Despite his youth, he became vicar to the bishop and deputised for him during the latter's absence in 1120 and 1121; clearly the young cleric was being groomed for higher things by the more senior churchmen. Next, he was sent to Lismore in Waterford, at that time one of the major centres of the ecclesiastical reform movement in Ireland. When the bishop of Down, the 'successor of St Comgall', died in 1123, Malachy was sent to Bangor to revive and reform the ancient monastery there, which had become increasingly secularised. In the following year he was also made bishop of the newly-constituted neighbouring diocese of Connor. It is said that he pursued all the tasks asked of him with great vigour until he was driven out of

Bangor by opponents in 1127. He returned to Lismore with some companions and set up a new monastery nearby, at an unidentified location called by his 'biographer', Bernard, *Ibracense.*

In 1129 the bishop of Armagh died. This was **St Cellach**, who had nurtured and promoted Malachy. Cellach had also been a great church reformer. He had overseen a major transformation of affairs in Armagh. Like many of the great ecclesiastical settlements in other parts of the country, Armagh had become increasingly secularised – to the point where senior 'church' offices had been monopolised by a particular family, the Clann Sínaich, for about 200 years. The actual incumbent of the highest position, the so-called 'successor of Patrick', was normally a lay man, who may or may not have had the appropriate spiritual qualities.

Like many of his predecessors, Cellach also had been a lay man when he was nominated to the position, but, conscious of the need for reform, he had himself ordained as a priest. His grandfather Mael Ísu, who died in 1091, had also been 'successor of Patrick'. Mael Ísu was succeeded by his brother Domnall, and on his death in 1105 the Annals of Ulster tells us, 'Cellach son of Aed son of Mael Ísu was appointed in his place to the successorship of Patrick by the choice of the men of Ireland, and he was ordained [a priest] on the feast of Adomnán [23 September].' The following year while on a visit to Munster, where church reformers were very active, and also 'by the command of the men of Ireland', Cellach 'assumed the orders of a noble bishop'. After his death, Cellach too was to be venerated as a saint. His feast day is 7 April. The *Annals of Ulster* gives him a fulsome, if somewhat exaggerated, obituary:

> Cellach, successor of Patrick, a virgin and the chief bishop of west-
> ern Europe, and the only head whom Irish and foreigners, lay and
> clergy, obeyed, having ordained bishops and priests and all kinds
> of clerics also, and having consecrated many churches and grave-
> yards, having bestowed goods and valuables, having exhorted all,
> both laity and clergy, to uprightness and good conduct, after a life
> of saying the hours [the holy office], saying mass, fasting, prayer,
> after being anointed and having made excellent repentance, sent
> forth his soul to the bosom of angels and archangels in Ardpatrick
> [County Kerry] in Munster on Monday 1 April, the twenty-fourth
> year of his abbacy and the fiftieth year of his age. His body was
> brought on 3 April to Lismore in accordance with his own testa-
> ment, and was waked with psalms and hymns and canticles, and
> buried with honour in the cemetery of the bishops ...

Before he died, Cellach had nominated Malachy as his successor. However, this appointment was opposed by those
who favoured the system of hereditary succession to this
important post. As St Bernard put it: 'they would not allow
anyone to be bishop unless he belonged to their tribe and
family.' As a result, Malachy was not able to take possession
of the See of Armagh until 1134. In 1137, however, having
successfully challenged the hereditary principle, he
resigned his post. This, apparently, was a diplomatic gesture
to his opponents. He resigned in favour of another reformer,
Gilla mac Liag or **Gelasius**, who, previously, had been
abbot of the Columban monastery of Derry. On Gelasius's
appointment, Malachy took up, again, the position of
bishop of Down. Gelasius, who was born in 1087 and died
in 1173, was also venerated as a saint. His feast day was 27
March.

Late in 1139 or early the next year, Malachy set out for
Rome to try to obtain full papal approval for organisational
reforms in Ireland, and in particular to secure full recogni-
tion as archbishoprics of the sees of Armagh and Cashel. He

travelled by way of Scotland and York. On the way, in March 1140, he visited St Bernard's monastery at Clairvaux in France. It appears that he was so taken by the way of life he found there that he himself wished to become a Cistercian monk, but was refused permission to do so by the pope, Innocent II, when he finally got to Rome.

Malachy failed also in his mission to have the archbishoprics officially recognised. Instead the pope appointed him papal legate to Ireland, urging him to return there and to convene an appropriate synod at which the whole Irish church might unanimously demonstrate its desire for the two archiepiscopal sees. Malachy returned via Clairvaux, this time leaving four monks from his own community behind to be trained as Cistercians. He also visited the Augustinian abbey of Arrouaise, near Arras in Flanders, and likewise left monks there to be trained in that form of monasticism.

Shortly after his return to Ireland, and the return of the four Irish monks from Clairvaux, in 1142, he established the first Cistercian monastery in the country, at Mellifont Abbey in County Louth. The first Augustinian community was set up at St Mary's Abbey in Louth about the same time, with the patronage of Malachy. At that time Louth was part of the kingdom of Airgialla (anglicised as Oriel) and its king, Donchadh O'Carrol, was a strong supporter of Malachy. Malachy continued the work of reforming the church and called together the Irish church council suggested by the pope.

In 1148 he set out for Rome again, to seek papal approval for the archbishoprics, armed now with the formally endorsed wishes of the rest of the Irish clergy. Once again he travelled via Clairvaux, but this time he took ill there and died, allegedly in the arms of St Bernard. Malachy was fifty-four years of age at the time of his death. He was buried beside the high altar in the abbey church at Clairvaux.

Immediately after he died, Bernard began to write the Life of Malachy, and also began the promotion of his cause for canonisation. St Bernard is reputed to have continued to wear Malachy's vestments on special occasions as a mark of honour for some time after his death. After his own death, St Bernard was buried close to his friend. As its translator Brian Scott pointed out, the Life of Malachy was the only such work that St Bernard wrote, a testament to his admiration and affection for the Irishman whom he cannot have known terribly well. Bernard is not always very complimentary when it comes to his descriptions of the Ireland of the time. His opening lines are reminiscent of the remark often attributed to the Duke of Wellington, who is said to have pointed out, when asked if he was an Irishman, that the fact that Jesus had been born in a stable didn't make him a horse:

> Our subject Malachy, born in Ireland of a barbarous people, was brought up and educated there. But he contracted no taint from the barbarism into which he had been born, any more than the fish of the sea do from their native salt.

Malachy was canonised in 1190 by Pope Clement III. His feast day was established on 3 November to avoid the Feast of All Souls on 2 November, the actual date of his death.

Malachy did not leave any writings behind him. The so-called *Prophecies of St Malachy,* which purport to predict, in the form of riddles, future popes as well as other innovations, are 'forgeries' of a much later date, like the similar *Prophecies of St Colum Cille.*

16. St Laurence O'Toole

St Laurence O'Toole (Lorcán Ua Tuathail) was born in 1128, apparently near Castledermot in County Kildare. His father, Muircertach Ua Tuathail, was chieftain of the local petty kingdom of Uí Muiredaig (now represented by south Kildare), itself a part of the larger kingdom of Leinster. Laurence's mother belonged to another north Leinster aristocratic family, the O'Byrnes from Wicklow. From 1132, the king of Leinster was Dermot Mac Murrough (Diarmait Mac Murchadha), himself to acquire a (not entirely deserved) notorious reputation in Irish history, as the person who brought the Anglo-Normans here. Around 1153, Dermot would eventually marry Laurence's half sister, Mór.

At about ten years of age, Laurence was sent to Dermot's household as a hostage of his father's loyalty to the overking. Hostage-taking such as this was a normal part of contemporary Gaelic social custom, and at first Laurence was treated as well as any member of the king's own family. However, as relations between his father and Dermot deteriorated, Laurence was, effectively, made a prisoner, 'in a desert, stony place'. After about two years of this harsh treatment, the abbot of Glendalough mediated on his behalf and, probably in the year 1140, was allowed to take Laurence under his care at the famous monastery in the middle of the Wicklow mountains.

Laurence remained at Glendalough for about twenty-two years, gaining a reputation for learning and piety. Around 1150 he was appointed abbot of the monastery, which had been founded by St Kevin 600 years earlier. During his abbacy Laurence founded the Priory of St Saviour's, just to the southeast of the main settlement at Glendalough.

St Saviour's was an Augustinian monastery, following the Arrouasian rule. Arrouasian monks lived a disciplined life – for example, they had a rule of strict silence and ate no meat or fats. They take their name from the abbey of Arrouaise in Flanders, where they were first established, around 1090.

Also during his abbacy, Laurence declined the position of bishop of Glendalough. However, on the death of Gregory, archbishop of Dublin, in October 1161, Laurence was chosen to succeed him. His appointment both as abbot of Glendalough and as Archbishop of Dublin had been supported, if not actually engineered, by his former captor, King Dermot Mac Murrough, now one of his most important supporters.

Laurence's appointment in Dublin was a major innovation. Apart from the fact that he was the first person from a Gaelic background to be appointed to this office – Dublin was in origin a Viking settlement and for a long time maintained its separate Scandinavian character – his selection marked the end of the strong association, going back over 100 years, between the See of Dublin and the See of Canterbury in England. Laurence was consecrated the following year, 1162, in Christchurch Cathedral by Gelasius, archbishop of Armagh, the primate of the Irish Church. The impact of this ceremony was that Dublin, which had previously stood outside the ranks of the main ecclesiastical organisation in Ireland, was now fully absorbed into the structure of that church.

Laurence immediately set about introducing various reforms. Shortly after his consecration, he sent two Dublin monks to Rome to get authorisation for the chapter of Christchurch to adopt the rules of the Arrouasian Augustinians. In 1166 he witnessed the foundation by Dermot Mac Murrough of the Priory of All Hallows, located just outside the then eastern walls of the tiny city of Dublin.

All Hallows was another Augustinian monastery, and it might be worth pointing out that Dermot was the founder of several other such houses. Despite the fact that at his death in 1171 the *Annals of Ulster* states that he died 'without unction, without body of Christ, without penance ... in reparation to Colum Cille and Finnian and to the saints besides, whose churches he had destroyed', Dermot had been patron to a number of existing churches, as well as the founder of several other new monasteries. St Mary's at Ferns in Wexford – his own main dwelling place; St Mary de Hogges for canonesses in Dublin, together with its daughter houses at Aghade in County Carlow and Kilculliheen in County Kilkenny; as well as the Cistercian abbeys in Baltinglass, County Wicklow, and Killenny, County Kilkenny, all owe their foundation to Dermot.

The Priory of All Hallows in Dublin was dissolved in the sixteenth century and the site was granted by Queen Elizabeth I as the location for Trinity College when it was founded in 1591. The famous Campanile in the college's Parliament Square is said to be located on the site of the crossing-tower of the Priory church.

Although, as one of only four Archbishops in Ireland, Laurence was a very eminent churchman, we are told that he continued to maintain his various ascetic practices – living the life of a monk, including the wearing of a hair-shirt beneath his outer clothes. He also made a retreat each year in Lent, returning to his ecclesiastical roots in the monastery of Glendalough.

Despite his piety, he could not remain free of secular matters. In his important position, he inevitably became embroiled in political affairs. In 1167 he attended the convention at Athboy, County Meath, which recognised Rory O'Connor from Connacht as the high king of Ireland – the last person to be honoured with this title. Rory had come to power the previous year and one of his first acts had been the expulsion from Ireland of Dermot Mac Murrough. This was a fateful act as, when Dermot returned to Ireland in 1167, he brought with him a group of Anglo-Norman mercenaries. This was the prelude to the so-called 'Norman Invasion' of 1169. As part of this process, Dermot's daughter Aoife, a niece of Laurence O'Toole, was married to the great Norman leader Richard, earl of Pembroke, better known as 'Strongbow'.

The capture of Dublin became an important part of the Norman plan, and Laurence O'Toole became fully involved in the diplomatic negotiations surrounding this, as well as ministering to his terrified flock. Strongbow was soon followed by the King of England, Henry II, to whom Laurence paid due respect when he came to Dublin. In 1175 Laurence witnessed and partly negotiated the agreement reached between Henry II and Rory O'Connor, known as the Treaty of Windsor. This recognised Rory's authority in Ireland in the areas outside Norman control. In 1177, King Henry, with the approval of Laurence, established another Augustinian monastery just outside the western edge of the city. This was the Abbey of St Thomas the Martyr – dedicated to Thomas à Becket, in whose murder at Canterbury the king had been implicated.

In 1179 Laurence attended the third Lateran Council of the universal Christian Church in Rome and was appointed Papal Legate for Ireland by Pope Alexander III. The following year he left Ireland again, to visit Henry II on a diplomatic mission for Rory O'Connor. The King was reluctant to see Laurence and, from England, the Archbishop had to follow Henry to Normandy. While staying there, at the Augustinian Abbey at Eu, Laurence became ill and died. His tomb became a place of pilgrimage for many of his Irish contemporaries and, in 1191, the monks at Eu made an application for his canonisation. This was granted in 1226 by Pope Honorius III. Shortly afterwards a Latin Life of St Laurence O'Toole was written. His feast day is marked on 14 November and he is honoured as the patron saint of Dublin.

17. Blessed Thaddeus Mac Carthy and St Oliver Plunkett

Beatification is the first part of the process of canonisation. When an individual is beatified, the Roman Catholic Church affirms that he or she may be publicly venerated. Several Irish people have been beatified, with the causes for their fuller canonisation at differing stages. One of these is **Blessed Thaddeus Mac Carthy**, about whom not a great deal is known. He was born about 1455 into the well known Munster aristocratic family of that name and may have been the son of Cormac Mac Carthy Mór and his wife Eleanor. His Irish name may have been Tadhg, of which Thaddeus could be a Latin rendering.

It is possible that he was educated in Rome, for there, on 3 May 1482, he was consecrated Bishop of Ross, having received a papal dispensation from Pope Sixtus IV on account of his young age of twenty-seven. Confusion seems to have reigned – presumably this would have been normal at a time of very poor communications between Rome and Ireland – as, when the bishop got back to his County Cork diocese, he found that the see was already occupied, by one Hugh O'Driscoll. The matter got ever more complicated, with Thaddeus, apparently, being excommunicated on a number of occasions. Around 1488, Thaddeus went back to Rome, appealed to the pope and requested him to set up a commission of enquiry into the complicated problem. The commission found no wrongdoing on the part of Thaddeus and his excommunication was revoked. He was appointed instead as bishop of the adjacent diocese of Cork and Cloyne in 1490.

However, on his return to Ireland, he once again found the see occupied – this time by Gerald Fitzgerald, a member of the powerful Desmond family. Again Thaddeus set out for Rome. Having argued his case, he procured a document from the pope confirming his appointment and excommunicating Gerald Fitzgerald instead. Thaddeus set out on the return journey to Ireland, but at Ivrea, a town in the Piedmont district of northern Italy, he took ill. He died during the night of 24 October 1492.

A number of visions were said to have been seen at the time of his death. He was buried in the local cathedral, where his tomb became the centre of attraction for pilgrims. Various miracles have been claimed as a result of his intercession. When his tomb was opened in 1742, it is said that his body had remained uncorrupted. He was beatified – a first step in the process of canonisation – by Pope Leo XII in 1896 and became known as the 'White Martyr of Munster'. His feast day is 25 October.

St Oliver Plunkett was the last Irishman to be canonised. He was born at Loughcrew, near Oldcastle in County Meath, on 1 November 1625. He belonged to a family of minor Catholic landowners of Anglo-Norman descent, the so-called 'Old English'. His early education was attended to by a relative, Patrick Plunkett, abbot of St Mary's Abbey in Dublin and brother of the first earl of Fingall. In 1647 Oliver went to study in Rome, at the Franciscan Irish college which had been founded there in 1625. He was, by all accounts, an excellent student, especially in philosophy, theology and mathematics, but also in civil and canon law. He was ordained a priest on 1 January 1654.

These were particularly difficult years for Irish Catholics, in the aftermath of the Cromwellian persecutions and confiscations, and Oliver Plunkett successfully requested permission to stay in Rome. In 1657 he was appointed a professor of theology at the College of Propaganda Fide, where he continued to teach until 1669, acting also as a representative of the Irish bishops. On 9 July 1669 he was appointed archbishop of Armagh and primate of Ireland and was consecrated on 30 November that year, at Ghent in Belgium. On his way back to Ireland he stopped in London, where he attempted to use his influence to mitigate the effects of anti-Catholic laws on his fellow countrymen.

By March 1670 he was back in his diocese. He became very active in restoring church discipline after the disruption of the previous decades, and is said to have suffered severe hardships in his attempts to minister to his flock. In Drogheda he opened a high school which he staffed with Jesuits. He was on good terms with the most senior government official in Ireland, Lord Lieutenant Baron Berkely, in the years from 1670 to 1672. He used this contact to arrange for a number of so-called 'Tories' (outlaws) from Ulster to be allowed to leave the country and go into military service on the continent. This would later be used as a charge against him.

His endeavours were not welcomed by all the Catholics in Ireland. Some of the native Gaelic clergy were suspicious of his Old English background, not to say of his determination to enforce church rules and discipline. He evoked the anger of the Franciscans – many of whom came from a Gaelic background – by favouring the Dominicans in a clash about property in 1671. On the issue of whether Dublin or Armagh was the primatial see in Ireland, Oliver Plunkett clashed with the archbishop of Dublin, Peter Talbot. Each of them wrote defences of their respective positions: Oliver Plunkett's *Ius primatiale* was published in 1672 and Talbot, now in exile in Lille in France, published *Primatas Dubliniensis* in 1674. This was, to say the least, a very esoteric topic for a church which was coming under official government

persecution once again from 1673. Oliver Plunkett frequently had to go into hiding, and writs for his arrest were
issued repeatedly by the government in Dublin.

The crisis known as the Popish Plot in England in 1678
complicated matters further. The Popish Plot was an alleged
conspiracy of English Catholics to assassinate King Charles
II. It was, of course, a hoax, but it was taken very seriously in
England – over twenty people were executed as a result.
Reaction in Ireland was at first fairly restrained but, on 16
October 1678, a government proclamation was issued
closing all Catholic churches and schools, and banishing
bishops and members of religious orders from the country.
Some bishops and monks were jailed, among them Peter
Talbot, still Archbishop of Dublin, who later died in
custody.

Oliver Plunkett was captured also and was imprisoned
on 6 December 1679 at Dublin Castle, where he is said to
have given the last sacraments to his fellow prisoner, the
dying Archbishop Talbot. Plunkett was accused, amongst
other things, of planning an invasion from France. Among
those who gave evidence against him were several of the
disaffected Catholic clergy whom he had previously antago-
nised, including the former vicar of the Armagh Franciscans.

Oliver was brought to trial in Dundalk in July 1680, but
the case against him collapsed. He was transferred to
London, where the political situation at the time required a
major Catholic scapegoat. He was found guilty of the
charges brought against him and sentenced to be hanged,
drawn and quartered. Although the Popish Plot had by now
run out of steam, and the witnesses against Plunkett had
been discredited, king Charles II refused to grant him a
pardon. On 1 July 1681 he was taken under guard to Tyburn
and, in front of a vast crowd, executed. His remains were
buried in St Giles's churchyard, but early in 1684 they were

transferred to the Benedictine Abbey at Lambspring in Germany. Two hundred years later they were brought back to Downside College in England. It appears that his head was enshrined from an early date. In 1722 it was returned to Drogheda, where it can still be seen.

Oliver Plunkett's name was added to the list of over 250 persons who it was claimed had died for the Catholic faith in England during the sixteenth and seventeenth centuries. In 1886, Pope Leo XIII approved their cause for beatification. Oliver Plunkett was declared 'blessed' in 1920 and in 1975 he was canonised, the first Irish saint in over seven hundred years. His feast day is 11 July (i.e. 1 July – the day on which he was executed – according to the revised calendar).

Modern Ireland is hardly an 'Island of saints' anymore, but traditional practices associated with many saints' cults are still widely observed around the country. Some of these have even had something of a renewal in recent times, often associated with the spread of 'new age' beliefs or the continuing human search for spirituality and meaning in life. In addition, the causes for beatification and canonisation of several other individuals from this country are still being pursued within the Roman Catholic Church. These include figures such as: Nano Nagle (1718–84), who founded the Presentation nuns in 1776; Mary Aikenhead (1787–1858), who founded the Irish Sisters of Charity in 1815; Edmund Ignatius Rice (1762–1844), who founded the Irish Christian Brothers in 1820; and the ascetic Dublin working man, Matt Talbot (1856–1925). It is clear that, in one form or another, the saints will still be with us for some time to come.

Select Bibliography

John Carey, Máire Herbert and Pádraig Ó Riain (eds.), *Studies in Irish Hagiography: Saints and Scholars*, Dublin, Four Courts Press, 2001.

de Paor, Liam, *St Patrick's World*, Dublin, Four Courts Press, 1993.

Kenny, JF, *Sources for the Early History of Ireland: Vol I, Ecclesiastical*, Columbia University Press, 1929, and Dublin, Pádraic Ó Táilliúir, 1979.

Scott, Brian, *Malachy*, Dublin, Veritas Publications, 1976.

Ní Mheara, Róisín *In Search of Irish Saints*, Dublin, Four Courts Press, 1994.

Ó Fiaich, Tomás, *Columbanus in his Own Words*, Dublin, Veritas Publications, 1974.

Ó Riain, Pádraig, 'Towards a Methodology in Early Irish Hagiography', *Peritia*, volume 1, pp. 146–59, 1982.

Ó Riain, Pádraig, 'Cainnech *alias* Colum Cille, Patron of Ossory', *Folia Gadelica*, pp. 20–35, ed. RA Breatnach, Cork University Press, 1983.

Ó Riain, Pádraig, *Beatha Bharra: St Finbarr of Cork: the Complete Life*, London, Irish Texts Society, 1994.

Plummer, Charles, *Vitae Sanctorum Hiberniae* (2 volumes), Oxford University Press, 1910.

Plummer, Charles, *Bethada Náem nÉrenn: Lives of Irish Saints* (2 volumes), Oxford University Press, 1922 and 1997.

Sharpe, Richard, *Adomnán of Iona: Life of St Columba*, London, Penguin, 1995.

Webb, JF, *Lives of the Saints* (including *The Voyage of Brendan*), London, Penguin, 1965.